OLD SALEM TAVERN, WINSTON-SALEM, N. C., ARCHITECT UN-
KNOWN, 1784. *A landmark is a familiar thing on an otherwise lonesome path.
Is assurance worth preserving?*

THE RESTORATION MANUAL

An illustrated guide to the preservation
and restoration of old buildings

by Orin M. Bullock, Jr., F. A. I. A.

Drawings by the author unless otherwise credited
Written for the Committee on Historic Buildings
of The American Institute of Architects

with a Foreword by Morris Ketchum, Jr., F. A. I. A.

SILVERMINE PUBLISHERS INCORPORATED   NORWALK, CONNECTICUT

© 1966 by Silvermine Publishers Incorporated, William Wilson Atkin, President.

All rights reserved under International and Pan-American Copyright Conventions.

Published in U.S.A. by Silvermine Publishers Incorporated, Comstock Hill, Norwalk, Conn.

Published Simultaneously in Canada by Burns & MacEachern, Ltd., 135 Railside Road, Donn Mills, Ontario.

Manufactured in the United States of America.

ISBN 0—87231—009—4

Library of Congress Catalog Card Number 66-15647.

First American Edition May 1966.

Second Printing 1971.

CONTENTS

FOREWORD

Here is an invaluable introduction to a very special world of architecture—the restoration of historic buildings. Those enthusiastic and intrepid architects who venture into this world must be prepared to utilize "a careful and inquiring mind" in scientific exploration of history, archaeology, craftsmanship, equipment, economic feasibility of restoration and future use of the building or groups of buildings proposed for rescue and revitalization.

The complex technicalities of investigation, research, program, working drawings and specifications, execution and maintenance of such projects form, in themselves, a specialized art and science.

Starry-eyed enthusiasm is not enough. Endless patience and untiring perseverence are the necessary ingredients of success.

The basic decisions involved affect not only the building or buildings themselves but also the contemporary community of which they are a vital element.

In these days of unlimited urban growth, of changing social and economic patterns, we cannot hope to save every architectural fragment from the past. We must strive, instead, for an imaginative blending of old and new, past and present, in order to add diversity and spice to the cityscape. So treated, historic restoration, preservation and reconstruction are important elements in urban design.

What shall we strive to save? History? Souvenirs of famous events? Purity of style in architecture? What should we do with the structure? Restore it, relentlessly, to its earliest state? Turn it into one more museum?

Any or all these values and possibilities may be involved but the fundamental objective is to save architectural excellence, not architectural mediocrity. We cannot afford to destroy the few examples of excellence that have been left to us.

Our cities desperately need variety and delight, not merely in the idiom of one era or moment, but the expressions of variety and delight which have been provided by different men at different times in our country's development. Heaven knows we have little enough of antiquity and visible tradition; we must protect what remains of this heritage against the bulldozer and its master, the land speculator.

The public must be taught to understand that the past is an essential element of the future of our cities rather than something to be used up and thrown away in the name of progress.

To convince them, preservationists must not exaggerate their claims. They must limit themselves to the best buildings and neighborhoods and to selective instead of wholesale urban conservation.

We do, in fact, have a rich heritage. It lives in Georgetown, Jackson Square, Beacon Hill, Brooklyn Heights, Charleston, South Carolina and many another priceless historic area. In saving this heritage, architects must avoid both the lifelessness of the museum and the preciousness of make-believe. They must weave past and present together to create the living fabric of our cities.

In the firm conviction that support of this objective is a vital function of our professional society, The American Institute of Architects has sponsored the production and publication of this manual. It is our hope that it may prove to be an effective weapon in creating cities which inspire man's knowing and deliberate participation in the history of his day and age and thus enrich both his mind and his heart.

Morris Ketchum, Jr., FAIA, President
The American Institute of Architects

ROBIE HOUSE, CHICAGO, ILLINOIS, FRANK LLOYD WRIGHT, ARCHITECT, 1909.

ACKNOWLEDGEMENTS

The Committee on Historic Buildings of the American Institute of Architects sought for many years to encourage the writing of a text book on how to do a restoration. This manual is the result of their appointment of a sub-committee to direct such a work and the designation of the author to write it at their meeting in Philadelphia in the Spring of 1961. The editorial sub-committee was under the enthusiastic and capable leadership of Earl H. Reed, FAIA, chairman and included; John B. Cabot, AIA, Chief Architect, National Park Service; Robert C. Gaede, AIA, then Chairman of the Committee on Historic Buildings; A. Edwin Kendrew, FAIA, Senior vice-President of Colonial Williamsburg; Charles E. Peterson, FAIA, Committee on Historic Buildings; and, Joseph Watterson, FAIA, then Editor of the *Journal of the American Institute of Architects.* This sub-committee provided, out of their broad experience, the policy guiding the development of the original outline for the manual and generously devoted their time to a critical review and comment on the subsequent drafts of the manuscript.

Technical and editorial comments were freely provided by Henry A. Judd, Supervising Architect, Historic Structures, of the Eastern Office, Design and Construction, National Park Service and by Lee H. Nelson, Architect in that Office as well as by Charles W. Lessig, Architect, and Worth Bailey, Architectural Historian also of the National Park Service. Robert J. Piper, AIA, then Director of Professional Practice of the American Institute of Architects' staff, reviewed and made constructive suggestions on the sections dealing with specifications and contracts; George E. Pettengill, Hon AIA, Librarian for the American Institute of Architects was of material assistance in helping to compile and check the bibliography; Mrs. Frances H. Moltenberry, Research Historian, saved the author many hours reviewing published work on restoration; Mrs. Faynetta E. Nealis, then Staff Executive for the AIA Committee on Historic Buildings maintained constant executive pressure and encouragement on the author to "keep working", and Miss Lisa Hayward spent endless hours typing not only from obscure manuscript but from dictaphone tapes all of which she transformed into clear typscript.

Thanks are also due The Building Research Institute and the authors; Perry E. Borchers, Charles W. Lessig, Jack E. Boucher, Edgar B. Boynton, and Frank A. Smith, III for their permission to republish their technical papers which first appeared in *Building Research;* and to the National Park Service, Eastern Office Design and Construction for the use of material selected from their Historic Structures files; as well as to the Library of Congress for the use of drawings from the Historic American Buildings Survey files.

The author owes a particular and special debt of gratitude to his wife, Lucy Meadowcroft Bullock, and his daughter, Amanda, for their patience and understanding of the need for the major inroads on our private time for the writing and illustrating of this manual.

O. M. B. Jr.

HEXAGONAL CUPOLA, PEM-
BROKE COLLEGE CHAPEL,
CAMBRIDGE: CHRISTOPHER
WREN, ARCHITECT, 1664.

INTRODUCTION

The purpose of this manual is to indicate the basic procedure which should be followed in the execution of a commission to "restore" a building. The techniques outlined apply in general to the restoration of structures of any period, in any location, and of any magnitude. The specific techniques or special skills required must be adapted to each project. The difference between the restoration of a town and of an individual structure of the same cultural background and date will be principally a matter of organization and degree. All of the steps outlined and investigations discussed do not apply equally to all projects but they should all be given consideration and not summarily dismissed.

Restoration, used architecturally, means putting back as nearly as possible into the form it held at a particular date or period in time. Its accomplishment often requires the removal of work which is not "of the period." The value of a restoration is measured by its authenticity.

Preservation means stabilizing a structure in its existing form by preventing further change or deterioration. Preservation, since it takes the structure as found, does not relate to a specific period in time and is, architecturally, the most intellectually honest treatment of an ancient monument.

Reconstruction means the re-creation of a building from historical, archaeological, and architectural documents and other evidence, often highly conjectural. Parts of buildings which are "restored" often must be reconstructed because original work has been removed or changed; this detracts somewhat from the accuracy and possibly from the intellectual honesty of the restoration.

1

THE ARCHITECT

The architect fortunate enough to be awarded a commission to restore an ancient building should be one who has a careful and inquiring mind. He must be able to subordinate his own design ideas to the taste of past generations; he must resist at all costs the natural tendency to become enamored of any one particular period, style, or architectural idiom; he must leave no stone unturned in finding out all there is to know about the building and in restoring exactly what existed in it during the period selected for preservation. Every part should, if possible, be provably authentic, facilities and services necessary to present-day use, such as plumbing, climate control, electrical work, fire protection or alarm devices, should be unobtrusive. The architect must be interested in research because it is essential that he become as familiar as possible with life, manners, background, taste, and aspirations of the various generations who have inhabited or been associated with the building in order to reach accurate conclusions.

The ever-present problem confronting the architect, restorer, or sponsor, which must be resolved through a careful evaluation, is the reason for undertaking the project at all and the result which is desired. It may be assumed that the fundamental reason for preservation is to bequeath to the future a reliable representation of the architecture of the past. The nineteenth century English restorationists who earned for themselves the reputation of "vandals" sincerely believed that all old buildings should be returned to that particular period in history which they themselves thought had been the most important. They often revealed great imagination and scholarly understanding of a past architecture, but in superimposing their ideas on older buildings which had been "modernized" from generation to generation through the years they changed or destroyed forever some of the best examples of eighteenth century English architecture.

The almost immediate reaction to restoration by preconceived ideas was a movement toward preservation which it may be argued is equally improper. There is however some validity to the thesis found in *The Goths and Vandals,* by Martin S. Briggs: "Restoration of Ancient Buildings . . . a strange and most fatal idea, which by its very name implies that it is possible to strip from a building this, that, and the other part of its history — of its life, that is — and then to stay the hand at some arbitrary point and leave it still historical, living, and even as it once was. . . . But those who make the changes wrought in our day under the name of restoration, while professing to bring back a building to the best time of its history, have no guide but each his own individual whim to point up to them what is admirable and what is contemptible; while the very nature of that task compels them to destroy something and to supply the gap by imagining what the earlier builders should or might have done. Moreover, in the course of this double process of destruction and addition, the whole surface of the building is necessarily tampered with; so that the appearance of antiquity is taken away from such old parts of the fabric as are left, and there is no laying to rest in the spectator the suspicion of what may have been lost; and in short a feeble and lifeless forgery is the final result of all the wasted labor."

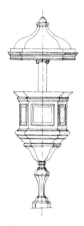

There is no formula which will provide an instant solution to the policy which should guide the preservation of any monument, each must be studied, investigated, researched and evaluated. The actual work done must not ever be capricious but should always be fully authenticated if the finished work is to have full value to the student of today and the visitor of tomorrow.

The architect for a restoration project should be responsible for the entire operation including historical, archaeological, and special research as well as the architectural work. Such centralization of responsibility will prove economical to the sponsor in the long run. Whether the architect has full charge of the work or not, it will still be necessary for him to coordinate and evaluate information and eventually recommend the exact scope of the project. His compensation, which must take into account this unusual breadth of service, may be based upon a percentage of the total cost of the work done under his jurisdiction or on actual costs incurred plus a fixed or percentage fee. Alternatively, the architect may be placed on the sponsor's payroll for the period

of the operation; in this case the sponsor himself may pay for such assistants, supplies, materials, and overhead as the architect requires in the conduct of the work, or he may reimburse the architectural office for its out-of-pocket expenditures on a periodic basis.

The architect will find all restorations are much more time consuming than new construction or alterations. His first few such commissions will be most frustrating unless he has a staff which has been trained in this field. Office assistants who are capable of understanding or detailing architectural features more ancient than those of 1920, (or who even display interest in finding out about older things) are exceedingly rare. In any event, every step of the restoration project must be under the close and meticulous supervision of the architect in charge. An error in judgment can cause irrecoverable loss of original portions of the structure and an error in design may result in the reconstruction of an unintentional fraud which will be taken for truth in years to come.*

---

*For a detailed discussion of Problems of the Restoration Architect Working Drawings, Specifications, and Bids, see *Building Research* Sept.-Oct. 1964 by James W. Burch.

TAYLOR HOUSE, RACINE, WISCONSIN, ARCHITECT UNKNOWN, 1853.

THE DEVELOPMENT
OF PROGRAMS

The proposed use of the building to be restored must be at least tentatively determined as soon as possible. It should be made with the guidance of the architect immediately after his study of its history and a superficial examination of the building.

Starry-eyed and enthusiastic sponsors enamored of the history or architectural character of a building may derive tremendous personal satisfaction and pleasure from its restoration and preservation. But unless there is a definite plan for use, one which will by income or endowment provide the necessary funds for its operation and maintenance, their enthusiastic zeal will probably die with them.

Potential sponsors of restoration projects must keep in mind the solid economic fact that it takes a great many "silver offerings" to maintain any structure. It is also unfortunately true that only an exceptional building, perhaps associated with a nationally known and beloved figure and located in a convenient place, will attract even a reasonably large number of paying visitors.

Old buildings have been restored and preserved primarily to house memorabilia accumulated by historical groups and societies. Others have been restored and are preserved as museums, with or without interpretation programs. Still others have been restored and are used for the purpose for which they were designed.

The use to which the restored building is put should be as compatible as possible with the intention of the original builder and designer. Thus it is logical to restore a courthouse for that use if there exists a need for a courthouse of that size in that location. A residence, large or small, will be best

5

CYRUS SKINNER'S SA-
LOON AND HOTEL,
BANNACK, MONTANA,
ARCHITECT UNKNOWN,
C. 1862.

preserved if continued in use as a residence. (The Society for the Preservation of New England Antiquities for instance, has worked out a number of leasing arrangements which provide for the use and exhibition of buildings by private individuals. The agreement insures their preservation in perpetuity while serving the dual purpose of public education and private accommodation.)

Structures which cannot continue to be used for their original purpose will, through their room arrangement, size, and location suggest other modern uses which may prove to be adequate economically. Offices, shops, information centers, society headquarters, country clubs, little theatre groups, and many other functions may be considered; the list is endless.

The problem of establishing a use to which an old building may be put after its restoration is actually not unlike that confronting an investor in any commercial enterprise except that the latter has a particular type of building and use in mind and can make an evaluation on that basis. The potential sponsor for a restoration project, on the other hand, may find it necessary to investigate the entire field of human endeavor before reaching a decision. His analysis of possible uses should be determined on fundamental guidelines.*

*See also National Trust Leaflet, "Criteria For Evaluating Historic Sites and Buildings."

RIO RANCH HOUSE,
SAN MIGUEL, CALI-
FORNIA, ARCHITECT
UNKNOWN, C. 1850.

First, the historical or architectural importance of the structure: national, state, local; important individual, important event, other social significance; a unique architectural example of a period, the work of a great architect.

Second, the size of the structure and the disposition of its rooms.

Third, the location of the structure: city, town, or country; accessibility to people; availability of supporting or auxiliary facilities.

Guided by these basic considerations the economic potential may be evaluated. Bear in mind always that even though a project must remain solvent, it is undertaken primarily to preserve a part of our architectural and/or cultural heritage for posterity. Do not consider "cutting corners" in design research or execution.

While making a study of possible uses for the building, consideration must be given to the consequent requirements and possible effect on the historic value of the architecture as it still exists in original form. For example, an old structure which has been entirely changed on the inside during the course of its history and retains practically no original work, may be worthy of restoration on the exterior only, permitting complete latitude for the redesign of the interior. This may be particularly true of a building which has no special historical significance. On the other hand, it is sacrilegious to destroy original "period" interior work, in a building rich in social history, to effect the alterations required for a modern use. In such a case, only those uses should be considered as can be reasonably well accommodated within the existing arrangement of rooms, without changing their architectural character.

An early determination of the possible use to which a building may be put is essential to guide the direction and scope of the architectural examination. (Those who restored the Boston home of Paul Revere to a period before he was born may have given posterity an example of early Boston architecture but they no longer can present Paul Revere's house.) At this stage it may be found that certain suggested uses will be unacceptable because of the inability of the old structure to accommodate the mechanical equipment required without serious damage to its architectural character.

A cultural historian sponsor will normally seek to have a restored building provide the background for the presentation of a particular period in history, a great event, or a famous person. On the other hand, an architecturally-minded sponsor will be more interested in attempting to preserve a building as it is found, retaining the changes to which it has been subjected by the varying tastes and preoccupations of its owners or occupants over many gen-

7

erations. Such a decision may result in a background against which the lucid presentation of history is difficult. The fact that many people are interested in specific times and events has influenced the sponsors of most restorations to select particular periods in time for restorations. The ethics of restoration to some selected time in history may be open to debate, but it has not been often that a building in this country has been preserved exactly as found.

The last and perhaps most elusive determination which will become a part of the program for a restoration is the date or period in time to which the building is to be restored. The selection should be made on the basis of complete research, historical, archaeological and architectural. Paradoxically the date selected will also indicate to a degree the extent of the architectural and archaeological investigations. Both of these examinations will destroy some of the existing features and it is obviously better to preserve *in situ* as much of the work of the selected date as possible.

A tentative date may be selected after a study of the preliminary research of the historian and superficial examinations by the archaeologist and architect. At this stage it is reasonable to suppose that the historical characters or events associated with the building are known, and many of the architectural features will have been identified. It should be possible to make reasonable

BURLINGTON COUNTY COURT HOUSE, MT. HOLLY, NEW JERSEY, SAMUEL LEWIS, MASTER CARPENTER, 1796.

TAVERN GUEST HOUSE, APPOMATTOX COURT HOUSE NATIONAL HISTORIC PARK. NPS PHOTOS. *This picturesque component of the complex aound the Tavern at Appomattox Court House was restored to the period of the Civil War rather than preserved with the remaining evidences of its service since c. 1819*

conjectures as to some specific physical features of architectural importance which existed at the time the events of history took place. Such a determination will make it possible to avoid disturbing much of the fabric which dates from the date tentatively selected.

It will be found in some cases that the importance of the architecture will outweigh that of political or personal history and the tentative date will be selected accordingly. Conversely in some houses the preservation should be directed to unusual or significant architectural features of a different period. (Such a determination will however present some problems in interpretation as is brought out in Chapter IX.)

In projects where architectural character is of primary importance the interests of architectural authenticity will be given precedence: no work dating from or before the period to be restored should be removed in the course of the architectural investigation or restoration. On the other hand, if the presentation of the building is to emphasize historical persons or events, the authenticity of anything but the surface visible on the date selected will be of less importance. A careful reconstruction may be as valuable as a setting for the presentation of history as a restoration even though the patina of age (that indescribable atmosphere) is removed and replaced by a modern finish.

when it was built. In spite of its checkered career evidence still existed to indicate its original appearance. Every feature of the restored building was confirmed either by architectural or archaeological evidence.

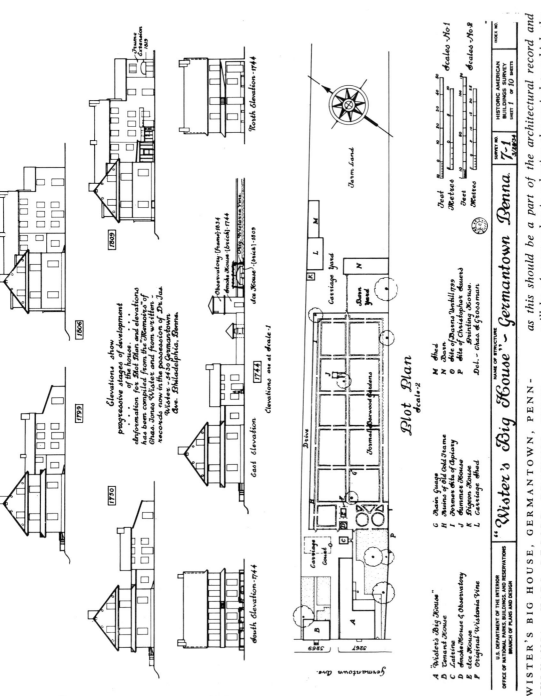

Elevations show progressive stages of development . . . . . of the house.

Information for Plot Plan and elevations has been compiled from the Memoirs of Chas. Jones Wister and from written records now in the possession of Dr. Jas. Wister - 5430 Germantown Ave. Philadelphia, Penna.

North Elevation - 1744

East elevation

Elevations are at Scale-1

Observatory (Frame) 1834
Smoke House (brick) - 1744
Ice House - (brick) - 1803
Orig. Wisteria Vine

1809

1806

1799

1750

South Elevation - 1744

Plot Plan
Scale-2

Drive

Carriage Court

Formal Boxwood Gardens

Carriage Yard

Barn Yard

Germantown Ave.

Farm Land

A "Wister's Big House"
B Tenant House
C Latrine
D Smoke House & Observatory
E Ice House
F Original Wisteria Vine
G Rain Guage
H Ruins of old Cold Frame
I Former Site of Apiary
J Summer House
K Pigeon House
L Carriage Shed
M Shed
N Barn
O Site of Barns (until) 1799
P Site of Christopher Sauer's Printing House.

Del. - Chas. L. Grossman.

Scales No.1
Feet
Metres

Scales No.2
Feet
Metres

U.S. DEPARTMENT OF THE INTERIOR
OFFICE OF NATIONAL PARKS, BUILDINGS, AND RESERVATIONS
BRANCH OF PLANS AND DESIGN

NAME OF STRUCTURE
"Wister's Big House" ~ Germantown Penna.

SURVEY NO. 7-1
HISTORIC AMERICAN BUILDINGS SURVEY
SHEET 1 OF 10 SHEETS
INDEX NO.

WISTER'S BIG HOUSE, GERMANTOWN, PENN-SYLVANIA. HABS RECORD DRAWING SHOW-ING GROWTH FROM 1744 TO 1806. COURTESY OF THE LIBRARY OF CONGRESS. Such a drawing as this should be a part of the architectural record and will be of great value in selecting the period to which the building is to be restored.

10

SELECTING THE PERIOD
TO BE RESTORED

Even though a tentative use and date for the restoration of a building must be known early in the execution of a project, every detail cannot be finally determined until all research and investigation have been completed. The tentative selection is made before any sub-surface study and often before all documentary and archaeological evidence is available; it provides, however, a useful working basis until research is completed.

When the research work is complete the architect must prepare a detailed report which will correlate the results of research by the historian, the archaeologist, and the architectural investigators. The report, illustrated by drawings and photographs indicating the initial construction, that of all subsequent periods, and the outstanding architectural features remaining, will provide the basis and the justification for the restoration of the entire project and all of its details. It will also include much of the background material upon which an interpretative program may be formulated.

It is very possible that after completing research and correlating the findings modifications should be made in the tentative program. For example, the architectural examination may show that practically none of the remaining work may be authenticated as being of the historical period selected, but that the building possesses architectural characteristics rare or important in the cultural history of the locality; then less emphasis may be placed on presentation of political or social history and more on its architecture. It may be an act of vandalism to strip away the architectural growth of one hundred and fifty years to effect a conjectural restoration of an original two-room cabin. On the other hand, the political significance of the site may be so great that it is considered essential to return the building to a particular decade.

While no hard and fast rules can be laid down for making such a decision, it seems sensible to give weight to the existence, in place, of authenticated architectural features and to set the date of the restoration at that period in time in which most of the existing fabric was built. The result will be a restoration which is also a preservation of as much of the authentic historic structure as possible. Generally speaking, preservationists agree that it is better to preserve than repair, better to repair than restore, and better to restore than to reconstruct.

At this stage, before working drawings are started, sponsors of the project and their technical advisors must arrive at a firm determination of the program for the use of the restored building, if possible space by space, but at least in a general way. Among the questions which must be answered are: (1) if it is to be a museum, what is to be exhibited, what period is to be interpreted, what operational and public facilities should be provided, what storage space or work space will be necessary, and what disposition is to be made of architectural features which were stripped from the building and will not be replaced; (2) if it is to be a place for public assembly, what are to be the size and purpose of proposed assemblages, and what necessary supporting facilities will be needed; (3) if for private organizational use, such as offices, what facilities will be required by this use; (4) if for modern public use such as a courthouse, record office, information center, what changes, if any, must be wrought in the ancient fabric. Obviously any and all of these uses must be considered in relation to the location of the structure and the possibility of providing supporting facilities in other buildings to minimize changes in the subject building.

Where little is known or remains of the interior of a building, its exterior restoration and reservation will be more important. In this case it may be more practical for modern use and less confusing to students to finish the interior in a contemporary manner. A period reconstruction if well done will not be distinguishable on the surface to even a practiced eye. In this event the record and interpretation must clearly report where the new work was done and the basis for its design.

MT. OVAL NEAR CIRCLE-
VILLE, OHIO, WILLIAM REN-
ICK ORIGINAL OWNER, 1832.

HISTORICAL RESEARCH

".......my system for a score of years past has been not to start with a preconceived theory and seek for its substantiation, but to — *let the evidence tell its own story.* Few workers on preconceived theories have been able to withstand for long the temptation to burke unreconcilable data. Approach the problem with an open mind and you are more likely to arrive at the truth."[*]

In restoration work the historian's research recovers the "story" of the site, information about the building, the people who built and those who used it, their lives, property, and personal possessions. It is the rare historical report, however, which includes an accurate physical description of the house or explains the exact nature of its contents. For this we must look to the archaeologist who may recover the physical remains which bring to life the mental picture created by the reports of the historian. Then the physical remains of the structure itself, its background and setting, must be studied and related to the information assembled by the historian and the archaeologist.

Through historical research may be found records establishing the date on which the building was built, by whom, for whom, and for what purpose. The records may also reveal the source of the materials and component parts used in the construction and even the dates certain items first became available; or they may give documentary clues which, when related to remains, offer provenance of fact. Obsolete or colloquial terms and names no longer currently used in the building industry, or phrases describing processes no longer followed often are understandable when related to discoveries made during architectural and archaeological examinations.[†]

---

[*]William Lawrence. "Pre-Restoration Stage Studies," Harvard 1927.   [†]See Glossary.

The extent of documentary source material available for historical research is literally endless and the accumulation of evidence related to a building and its uses can never be said to be absolutely complete. The following general areas should be investigated initially and will frequently suggest others:

Primary Sources include documents of public record like deeds, wills, contracts, agreements, indentures, vital statistics, maps, and census records which are found in Court Houses, Libraries, Title Guarantee Companies, Historical Societies, and in trunks and boxes stored in attics. They include insurance policies on the subject and adjacent property which are found in the archives of companies or libraries; private collections of family papers, which often contain drawings, letters,* journals, diaries, post-cards, photographs, stereoptican views, or inventories; commercial papers like store accounts, purchase orders, agreements, bills of lading, and even the private papers of friends, relatives, and neighbors. Oral evidences from knowledgeable old people will often provide a clue to clear up an obscure problem.

---

*In 1783, when the Revolutionary War was drawing to a close, General Washington was encamped with his troops at Newburgh, N. Y. He received a letter from his caretaker at Mount Vernon stating that the roof of the big mansion was leaking and asking for instructions. This was *General Washington's letter:*

"....I am truly unfortunate that after all the expense I have been at about my house I am to encounter the third Edition, with the trouble and inconvenience of another cover to it, after my return. That there can have been little attention, or judgment exercised heretofore in covering it is a fact that cannot admit a doubt; for he must be a miserable artizan or a very great rascal indeed who after one experiment could not tell what kind of shingles were necessary to prevent a common roof from leaking, or how to place them as they ought to be. Patience however and new exertions must supply these defects; & to prevent greater evils, the sooner the latter is applied the better; I desire therefore that a proper kind of Plank may bespoke to shingle upon — the thinner, provided the Nails do not draw, the better; as I am afraid of so heavy a weight on a slight foundation; for it is to be remembered that the Frame was for a one Story House and that every thing greater than that exceeds the original design. If New shingles are to be used, write to Mr. Newton to bespeak them; and let them be got full two feet in length, but I would submit to the workman if he has any skill in his profession, & the old shingles can be ripped off without Injury, whether shewing less of them will not supply the defect of their shortness — If it will, the Paint and Oil which has been expended on them will, in a great measure be preserved — but this is not to be placed in competition with a tight cover — or the look of the Work, if shewing little, become obnoxious to the view — When I suggest this idea, it is upon the principal that a short

Secondary Sources include published material related to the property, its development, use, and occupants. Footnotes in books can lead to additional sources, often primary. News stories, advertisements for lost property, items of sale, and reports on marriages, deaths, business ventures, or social activities may provide clues of the greatest importance. Bibliographies and indexes in public libraries, historical societies, and museums (public, commercial, and private) must all be investigated.

Peripheral Sources related to the period under study will include books, particularly architectural and carpenters' handbooks, trade catalogues, and business directories which were available to the owners, the designers, and the builders. Building codes governing construction, even tax laws and statutes passed by governing bodies having jurisdiction may reveal facts not otherwise in evidence. Complete legal specifications for public buildings have influenced, or been similar to, those written for nearby private work as to architectural design, methods of construction, availability of craftsmen, trade practices, and materials.

Sociological Data related to the period and region often provide information as to the availability of materials, and local methods of construction. The dates, for example, on which various manufactured products, such as nails, were available, whether hand wrought, cut, or wire; hardware, when circular sawn boards were first introduced, when various paint pigments, and particular sizes of window glass were available may be found in trade catalogues and national origin of the craftsmen who may have been employed, the travels of

---

shingle if it shews in proportion, affords as many laps as a long one, consequently (in a roof not very flat) must be as tight. For instance, if an 18 Inch shingle shews 6 Inches, two parts out of three of it is covered; so in a like manner is a 15 Inch shingle if it shews no more than 5 — But I think the proportion of the hidden part should be greater — for which reason with Shingles of two feet I would shew no more than 6 Inches — and with those now on the house if they are not more than 16, not more than 4½, which consequently renders it more difficult for the water to penetrate — It adds I grant to the weight because it takes more of the smaller sort or a greater quantity of Wood, if shingled with the larger, — but this is unavoidable — I again repeat, that no time is to be lost in redressing the present evil; for if it is suffered to continue, besides ruining the Plaster within, I shall have the furniture all spoiled; & remain in a scene of continual vesation & trouble till it is done. . . . .

Yr Affect friend,
G. Washington

the owners and their friends, and even their status symbols, furnishings, or memorabilia, may prove to be rewarding.

Techniques

Techniques for historical research must depend on the scope of the project but, no matter how apparently simple or obvious the problem, it is essential that complete notes be kept of all sources investigated, recording both positive and negative results. Without such a detailed record the same ground may be covered by subsequent researchers and even the original worker will be handicapped in attempting to prove, review, or check his work.

Subject cross indexes, maintained currently on slips or cards as the material accumulates will prove most useful. The assembly of historical information

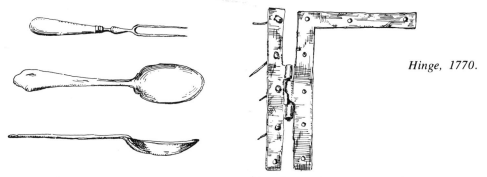

Hinge, 1770.

on an important property may occupy the time of many persons over many years and the index will be a welcome time-saving device long before the comprehensive historical report can be written.

Transcripts of records should be made verbatim, *never paraphrased;* often the original spelling of a word will provide a clue of vital importance. Microfilm, photostat, and duplicating equipment should be used whenever available to reduce the possibility of error and avoid the manual labor of copying. Accumulate and file full and complete information which is in any way related to the property under study. Record by reference all commercial, political, religious, military, and social activities indirectly related to the building and its occupants. Such information, while usually of no direct architectural importance will provide material for the presentation. The background and previous activities of the owners, designers, or builders often explains why they introduced an unusual feature, or may reveal the inspiration for the overall design.

Research notes relating to the site should be arranged chronologically, by the dates of the original documents in card files, letter files, or loose leaf binders depending upon the nature of the material, its size and volume, whether typescript, micro-film, photostats, or drawings. The filing system should be expandable to permit the addition of new items and must be available for review during its accumulation.

Door latch, 1827

The final index to the research records (which may not be essential to small projects) should be made in the greatest of detail, and include practically every noun, to permit the extraction of all information on a given subject without careful reading. Research records embrace various types of material which cannot be filed, stored, or bound in uniform size; for such records to be readily available, an index is essential. Include in the index references to bibliographies and source material not filed with the research records.

Research reports, in preliminary form, on subjects related to the site may be written after a substantial file of notes has been accumulated. The research historian (together with the archaeologist and architect) is cautioned to avoid drawing dogmatic conclusions and to restrict preliminary reports to facts until all of the archaeological and architectural investigations have been made. The meaning of many words found in the records such as "hall", "porch", "paneling", or "deal" should be interpreted with caution until their actual meaning has been positively proven.

The research library should contain as many original documents related to the property as possible, particularly books available to the owners and builders, drawings and models, photographs, and so on, not excluding books and documents related to the culture of the area and the origin of the building's inhabitants.

Research personnel may be professional or amateur. Because of the cost of professional research work and the impossibility of anticipating the time it will take, the amount of material which may be found, or the costs, reliance is often placed on amateur workers. Among those who may be helpful are antiquarians, history buffs, and women's organizations such as garden clubs and junior leagues. Every effort should be made to have a paid architectural historian direct the research on all but the smallest projects.

17

Laurel, Maryland.

ARCHAEOLOGICAL RESEARCH

Purpose

Archaeological exploration seeks to locate and identify the size and shape of buildings formerly on a site, to date and confirm the identity of structures, to trace the stages of their development and use, and to confirm or suggest the occupations and social status of their occupants. Archaeology is as essential to the restoration of an existing building as to one which has entirely disappeared. Buried remains may provide the only tangible evidence of the appearance of such features as steps, long ago replaced, wings or porches demolished, or cultural objects not identifiable by documentary evidence alone.

Archaeological exploration, therefore, produces two direct results: the first, physical remains of a building or parts of the physical remains, if they exist, and their former locations, if they are gone; and second, articles or remains of articles related to the building's occupants and their local activities.

The "site" on which the building under study stands may contain a treasure trove of artifacts and features which, when discovered, will provide information on the locations and uses of outbuildings, former occupancies, additions or changes to the principal building and provenance of the dates of its construction, physical evidence of lost architectural details, like hardware, and of the character of personal and household equipment used by the occupants. These may lie in garden beds or along paths, in the backfill of foundations or basements. Even fence-line roads, pathways, and changes in grade may be revealed by skillful excavation.

Details of the procedures to be followed will be governed by conditions on the site under investigation. Obviously the study of a city lot on which a his-

Hinge. 1776.

18

toric house is standing will differ from that of a country location or of one which has been radically changed through the years.

Excavation Procedure

This should take the following steps, adapted to the particular conditions, in order to minimize the danger of destroying archaeological evidence before it has been identified and recorded.

Normally, the remains of structures known as "features" are left in place, whereas the bits and pieces of artifacts are removed from the site. The removal of material from the context in which it was originally deposited is destructive of evidence. For this reason, the importance of careful procedure and meticulous keeping of records cannot be overemphasized. The same care should be taken on every site, regardless of its size.

A base map is needed on all but the smallest sites. This is made on a detailed topographic survey of the area to be investigated; plotted at fairly large scale it shows building locations, property lines, bench marks, and existing features, and is superimposed on a grid of convenient size — (say ten feet by ten feet).

The grid system should be staked on the ground itself and marked with the letters, numbers, and elevations which are shown on the base map. The grid stakes will be used to identify and locate notations of finds made which are recorded in the excavator's daily notebook.

Photographs of the site and every exposed feature should be made before any work is started, every time any change is made, such as when the grids have been staked out, when the ground cover (shrubs or trees) is cleared, and almost daily during excavation.

Spoil or waste storage is a logistic planning operation. Archaeological investigation involves digging holes in the ground and the result of digging is inevitably a pile of dirt, physical material which occupies space and must be disposed of somewhere, preferably not on a spot under which a feature is likely to be found at a later date. It is very frustrating to be forced to shift waste material from one place to another in order to clear the site on which to continue a "dig" which is following a feature, particularly if the shift has been caused by a lack of planning or foresight.

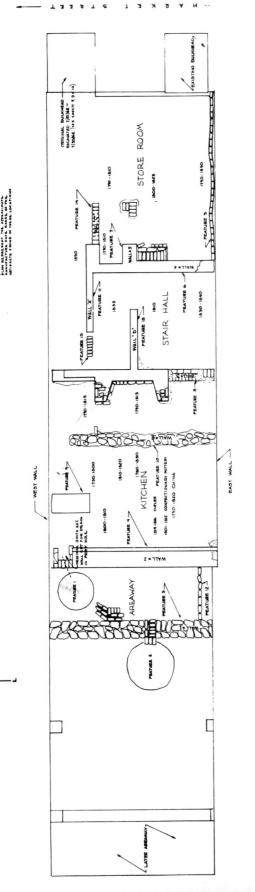

ARCHEOLOGICAL DATA FOR 322 MARKET STREET

BASEMENT FLOOR PLAN

HOUSE AT 322 MARKET STREET, PHILADELPHIA, PENNSYLVANIA.
NPS PHOTO. *Above and facing page Comprehensive excavation of areas under a building is often found necessary. Buried evidence reveals when uncovered, structure, plan, and the use of the space; as in this picture of a completed excavation looking south into the areas of the cellar stairhall. See also accompanying archaeological drawing of the excavation (facing page). The excavation plan from the archaeologist's report not only records the significant structural elements uncovered but the artifacts as well—where found, their identification, association, and their dates. NPS Drawing.*

21

Resist the impulse to get on with the dig until all of the available evidence has been gleaned from a study of the historical research, air photographs, old maps and pictures, surveys, etc., and the locations of all physical features to be investigated have been plotted on the base map and indicated by stakes on the site. Spoil may then be stored elsewhere. The probable existence of features which should be excavated but which are not apparent on the surface or whose location is not known, may sometimes be found by probing, or more effectively by digging test pits or cross trenches.

Probing with a pointed iron rod may reveal the approximate or probable location of structural remains which are mentioned in documents or are suspected of having existed, but which have disappeared from the surface. When the point of the iron rod, the probe, comes in contact with an object harder than soil, like stone, rock, brick, or shell it will be apparent to the prober and he may make note of the presence of a "foreign body." Experience will teach the prober to tell one foreign body from another and to make a reasonably close guess as to what his probe may have struck. He should bear in mind, however, that "one swallow does not make a spring", the discovery of what may be thought to be a brick or two is not necessarily the remains of a building foundation. The lines and areas probed, the depth of the penetrations and the apparent stone or masonry encountered, should be recorded in a daily notebook, referenced to the grid on the base map. When all productive probing has been done a pattern of sub-surface conditions *may* emerge from the plotting of probe notes on the base map which will permit the dig to be planned. Such probing is of little positive archaeological value, but is a widely used first step.

Test pits are, next to rod probing, the most economical sort of archaeological investigation and are usually dug when the location of features is known or strongly indicated. They may be dug in a pattern suggested by documentary evidence of building locations, by the probable presence of structures found by probing, or in a pattern suggested by site conditions. Test pits will, of course, provide far more accurate and detailed information about sub-surface conditions than may be discovered by probing. In fact, a series of test pits is often sufficient in itself to indicate the extent, date, and former occupations of a site. Test pits are usually about four feet by four feet and spaced to expose anticipated remains. They are dug from the surface down to undisturbed soil or until a foundation or other feature is uncovered. Test pits are archaeological excavations and should be dug with the same care as comprehensive excavations.

Cross trenching is most adaptable to a vacant site on which the locations of previous occupancies are widely scattered or not known. The direction in which cross trenches should be run is determined by the probable orientation of the remains: the trenches should be dug so as to intersect the remains. (In Colonial Williamsburg, for example, cross-trenching was done at a 45° angle to the streets, thereby encountering practically all existing remains.) Cross trenches are not normally dug very deep (they should be stopped when significant structural remains or features are encountered or when undisturbed soil is uncovered) and they need only be wide enough for convenient working; approximately two feet.

The distance between cross trenches is governed by the probable sizes of the structures which it is thought may be found on the site, their probable location, and the required thoroughness of exploration. For example, a field which is known from historical references to have been used throughout the years as a pasture, on which no buildings are ever known to have existed, may be said to have been adequately investigated if cross trenches are spaced twenty-five feet or even farther apart. On the other hand, the area immediately adjacent to or including a former farm complex, should be cross trenched at four or five foot intervals. One rule of thumb to follow on potentially rich sites is the length of a shovel handle from one trench to the next; the problem of spoil disposition rears its ugly head in a closer cross trenching operation, particularly if the trenches must be carried to any depth.

Comprehensive excavation removes practically everything from the site except "original" construction features such as pavements, steps, walls, and footings, and should be planned on the basis of the evidence found by probing, test pits, and cross trenching. This operation entails the excavation of the entire site to expose all structural remains which can be found, to identifiy each part, and to establish relative sequences and their dates. If more than one period of construction is encountered each must be identified and its date established. The spoil storage or disposal problem in this operation will be major because of the large quantity of earth which must be removed and will depend on the proposed treatment of the site. Will the exposed structural remains be built upon, will they be stabilized soon after they have been dug up, or will they be covered up again after they have been studied and recorded? Unless the site is to be back-filled, temporary protection from the elements should be provided because long-buried brick deteriorates rapidly when exposed to weather, particularly at winter temperatures.

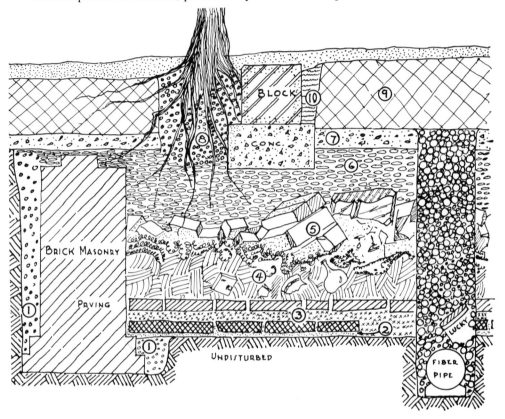

1. BACKFILL INCLUDING PIPE FRAGMENTS DATED c. 1680.
2. SAND & MARL IN WHICH WAS FOUND A COIN DATED 1650.
3. SAND-CLAY FILL CONTAINING BOTTLE BUTTONS DATED 1730.
4. DEBRIS FROM A FIRE – LOCKS, CHINA, BOTTLES DATING BEFORE 1750, COVERED WITH BLACK TOP SOIL.
5. ARCHITECTURAL DEBRIS INCL. MANTEL FRAGMENTS c. 1680.
6. WELL COMPACTED, UNIFORM CLAY FILL CONTAINING ARTIFACTS c. 1770.
7. MARL WALK IN WHICH WAS BURIED COINS DATED 1785 & 1800.
8. TREE PIT BACKFILL CONTAINING A YALE LOCK KEY.
9. FILL CONTAINING CHINA FRAGMENTS DATING FROM 1840.
10. BACKFILL CONTAINING A COCA COLA BOTTLE.

A hypothetical section through an excavation illustrating stratification and dateable finds which may establish the chronology of the several occupation periods.

24

Digging techniques will vary depending upon the type and state of soil involved, whether sandy, heavy clay, very rocky, disturbed or undisturbed, some digs will require shoring, some the use of pumps (if water is encountered), and some will work easily with shovel and trowel.

The excavation should be carried down, occupation layer by occupation layer (which may have been previously discovered and identified by the test pits or cross trenches) using such tools as the nature of the soil and number and stability of the artifacts or features encountered indicates. The excavation must be done with due care to insure the exposure, as near intact as possible, of all structural features and artifacts. The direction in which the excavation will progress and an understanding of the occupation of the site will be revealed as features and artifacts are recovered.

Record "balks" should be retained as long as possible in order to preserve for future reference and study evidence of the condition of the site before excavation. These unexcavated sections, usually about two feet thick, but varying with the nature of the soil should be left at convenient intervals throughout the excavation area. They reveal the stratigraphy, or cross sections, of the undisturbed earth on the site and serve as a check for the archaeologist and as an index to occupation levels. They may be permanent records available for future reference if allowed to remain intact when the dig is back-filled. Of course, if the building formerly on the site is reconstructed all original evidence of work will be lost forever. (The reconstructed "capitol" in Colonial Williamsburg is an exception; the original foundations, all that remains of the work of 1699 are still in place under the new building which is independently supported on a modern foundation system.)

Artifact is the generic term for all objects found by archaeological investigation. "Shards" or "sherds" which are broken pieces of pottery, china, or glassware, are perhaps the most common artifacts found, but the number and variety of others an excavator may anticipate recovering is as extensive as the cultural objects in possession of those who have ever had occasion to be on that particular spot: fragments of pottery, coins, children's toys, gardening tools, buttons, and any and all of the things both large and small used by man eventually find their way into the ground where they later provide mute evidence of the fact and time of his presence.

Artifacts have, throughout the years, been assessed at differing values by collectors, antiquarians, and archaeologists. Practically everyone enjoys collecting things; seashells, pebbles, bird's eggs, china, glassware, string, or mili-

TOP, SKATE WHEEL IN TANDEM, 1850. IMMEDIATELY ABOVE, WHALE OIL LAMP, EARLY 19TH CENTURY: FLINT GLASS.

tary objects. Sites of Indian occupations and old battlefields have been surface investigated and often dug for the primary purpose of recovering collector's items. A collector who knows where each of his arrowheads was found, and in what context, is indeed rare. Yet an unorganized collection, however beautifully mounted and displayed, is of little scientific significance.

All man-made objects or objects related to man should be identified if possible as they are uncovered, and the exact location and context in which they are found recorded.

The latest, or most recently manufactured article found in any stratum will establish a date for that stratum. This assumption can be upset because for one reason or another, holes in the ground are constantly being dug, and then back-filled, either with the same material re-deposited in inverse order from its removal or with material from an altogether different site. Careful excavators will recognize such holes as they dig and may even find them a valuable clue to the history of the site, rather than a frustration.

The condition of artifacts when recovered may be expected to vary all the way from an indistinguishable lump which may look like clay, iron ore, or rock to a coin in mint condition or a complete fire-arm. Obviously the nature of the material of which the object is made, is the largest contributing factor to its preservation. On the other hand, even material such as wood or leather, which deteriorates relatively quickly in the ground, has been found in perfect condition after hundreds of years of immersion in a wet or damp deposit. Often, important clues to the use of a site may be deducted by determining whether the object was deliberately disposed of as domestic trash or rubbish, was lost, thrown away, abandoned by its owner, inadvertantly used as fill material, or was waste material from an earlier excavation. (Material found

26

in the back-fill of builders' trenches, packed around posts, or in the filling of a well are examples of inadvertent movement of artifacts.)

Identification of artifacts is essential even though it may appear that the most important function of an archaeologist is to discover physical remains of structures which formerly occupied a site. He cannot begin to do justice to the investigation nor contribute his full share to the obtainable history of the site unless he makes full and complete use of the artifacts recovered.

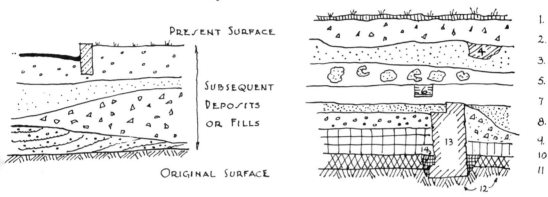

Stratification of the earth's surface is a natural geological phenomenon complicated by man-made disturbances. The accurate identification of each layer or strata through the excavation will reveal or supplement the story of occupancy on the site.

The drawing on the left indicates a possible accumulation on an original surface by natural means including a layer of silt deposited by flooding, a layer of leaves and organic debris, one of sand and clay, and finally one of topsoil into which a roadway has been cut. The undisturbed nature of the accumulation may be identified by the absence of man-made objects in the strata other than those associated with the roadway.

The other drawing indicates a possible accumulation on a site once occupied by a building. The excavator might uncover:

1. *Grass and topsoil*
2. *Hard packed soil*
3. *Sand Clay*
4. *Domestic Trash*
5. *Demolition rubbish, brickbats, etc.*
6. *Clay and decayed wood in the form of a post*
7. *Hard packed, clean, clay, apparently undisturbed*

8. *Silt and sand*
9. *Structural fire debris*
10. *Demolition debris*
11. *Hard packed soil*
12. *Sand shale clay*
13. *Masonry structural remains*
14. *Soil back fill*

The absence of artifacts in layer 7 might discourage further excavation and result in a failure to discover the earlier structural remains lying below. The presence of such clean fill well compacted is not unusual having been removed by equipment from excavations for modern work and placed here to provide another useable site.

27

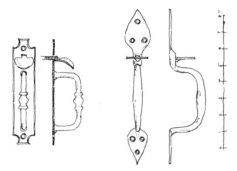

These thumb latches which were found in Santa Barbara, California are hardly distinguishable from east coast examples.

For this reason it is essential that the archaeologist employed to dig a site be thoroughly familiar with the people and cultural objects related to the period and area under investigation before beginning excavations. An Egyptologist or a student of American Indian mounds may be an excellent excavator but he might completely ruin an eighteenth century colonial site because he probably would fail to recognize and *identify* the vital clues as they were uncovered. Such knowledge is necessary because even fragmentary artifacts are often of great significance and to be of maximum worth should be recognized and identified in context at the time of discovery. Once they are removed, much physical evidence is lost. It is not enough for an excavator to know *only* the important or usual objects of the period: those which have enjoyed a short identifiable life span, such as commemorative plates or campaign medals, provide excellent dating evidence and the year of the first appearance of even common objects like wine bottles will help to establish the earliest possible date of the stratum in which they are found. Even though the exact nature or importance of an artifact may not be known or appreciated at the time of its excavation, subsequent study in the laboratory may reveal its value to the project.

An archaeological laboratory and store house is essential to the archaeologist for any site. He must be provided with ample space for the storage, processing, and analysis of the artifacts recovered. It is impossible, however brilliant or well-trained the director and the excavators may be, to extract the full value of the project from the artifacts as they are brought from the ground. The space required for this storage and laboratory work will vary with the site, the nature of its occupation, and the length of time it was occupied. A good rule of thumb for planning purposes is to make the archeological storage and laboratory space for excavation of a domestic site approximately the same size as the building being investigated.

If a laboratory staff is available the artifacts should be given initial processing at once, or very soon after their excavation; but if further investigation must be delayed for any appreciable length of time, the paper-bagged artifacts should be carefully deposited in wooden boxes, suitably identified, keyed to the excavation register, and stored. Adequate packing, permanent identification, and careful storing are all essential because artifacts placed in storage for future reference may remain for years before being given further attention.

The minimum equipment necessary in a laboratory includes sinks with hot and cold water and large tables on which artifacts may be spread and sorted. The maximum equipment desirable in an archaeological laboratory might include almost as much as that in a chemical or physics laboratory. The sophistication of the laboratory is, of course, governed by the size and scope and nature of the archaeological project, the nature of the artifacts recovered, and the uses to which they are to be put which might be study, exhibition or models for reproduction.

The minimum treatment for each recovered artifact, however small, should include washing and cleaning for identification and permanent marking with its registration number. Laboratory work may proceed from here to include thorough cleaning and a preservative treatment of those objects, such as iron, wood, or leather, which would otherwise continue to deteriorate in open air. Items of particular importance of which a sufficient number of fragments have been found, such as chinaware, pottery, and glassware, might be restored.

After the preliminary cleaning and marking for identification, artifacts should be sorted by stratum in which found. Their identification will help to establish the dates of the stratum and record the nature of the cultural objects found from each period. Similar artifacts may then be grouped together in an attempt to reconstruct or identify individual objects and further clarify the cultural history of the site.

Record of artifacts. As it is discovered, each artifact should be identified, if possible, and entered in an "excavation register" or note book giving the date, location on the site as related to the grid system, and elevation or stratum from which recovered. If the artifact is large or significant, it should be partially cleaned and carefully uncovered to permit a photographic record *in situ* before it is actually removed from the ground.

When removed, the artifacts should be bagged in heavy brown paper bags marked with the date recovered, the location of the site, and the registration

29

number; the bag contents should be recorded in the excavation register. Artifacts may be grouped if their size permits but care should be taken to keep material from various contexts in separate bags. Less significant artifacts, such as bits and pieces of china or glassware, unidentifiable lumps of rusted metal, bottle parts, and so on, must also be saved and deposited in marked bags; it is unwise to discard any artifact at this stage unless it is perfectly obvious that it has no connection with the site under study (a pop bottle for example). The paper bags, should be gathered up daily and taken to the laboratory or storage room.

Artifacts too large to be accommodated in paper bags or in storage boxes should be identified with firmly fastened tags of relatively imperishable material. All markings on bags, tabs, artifacts or storage boxes should be done in the most permanent manner possible; or the entire purpose of the archaeological exercise will be lost.

Significant artifacts can, after cleaning, preservation, and restoring, be used as part of the presentation and interpretation of the site to visitors. Actual pieces of the hardware used in the original building may thus be available for study and reproduction. Examples of the china, silver, and other articles of household furnishing which have been mentioned by name in inventories or wills may be identifiable in the collection. Even the quality and nature of carriages formerly stored in the stable have been positively identified from fragments of horse and carriage furniture recovered from the ground. Former residents' taste in wine and liquors and the source of their supply may be proved by remains of bottles. Clothing styles will be indicated by buttons or buckles or shoes.

Publication

The sponsor of an archaeological excavation project has a responsibility, and opportunity, far beyond the restoration of the particular site in which he is interested. The dissemination of archaeological information through the publication of reports is essential to the science and every sponsor should make sure that his archaeologist publishes a detailed report of his investigation as a part of his contract. Such reports are practically the only records of the gradual transition in form and design of many of the common everyday ob-

30

jects used by our forefathers. Through study of such reports of digs in various parts of the country, archaeologists become increasingly efficient in the interpretation and dating of evidence recovered in their own investigations.

A GREEK REVIVAL HOUSE, ST. PAUL, MINNESOTA, C. 1850.

THE CHARLTON HOUSE, WILLIAMSBURG, VIRGINIA, C. 1772. *Before restoration. Additions and modernizations through the years supplemented by neglect during modern times often combine effectively to mask the character of the original building.*

32

ARCHITECTURAL RESEARCH

Purpose

The objective of architectural research is to determine the character and date of a building and all its parts. This will include identifying the several periods of its construction and of all modifications, additions, and changes that have been made, as well as the order of their occurrence. It should provide the information on which to base recommendations for a restoration period or date. It will also identify the architectural details which will be incorporated in the working drawings.

Before the actual fabric of the building is studied, the architect must become conversant with all authenticated source material related to the structure, the site, its builders, owners, and occupants. Restoration is not a function of architectural imagination and original design, but one of accurate identification, understanding, and replacement. For this the architect must be familiar with the people, architecture, and culture of the period. Background material to be studied must include:

(a) Historical and archaeological reports for documented dates of initial construction, and of all subsequent changes or additions, pictures, descriptions, bills of materials, artifacts, and all references to the activities of the owners and builders.

(b) Precedent buildings, those of the same or approximate date in the immediate vicinity, as well as those in areas of similar culture and background which might have had an effect on the design, methods of construction, or craftsmanship employed in the erection of the subject building.

33

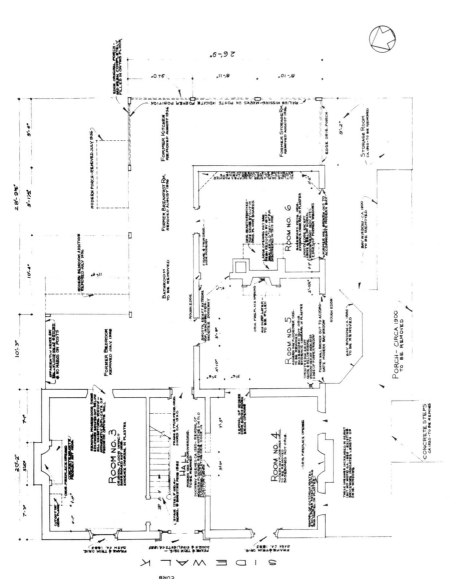

ANDREW JOHNSON RESIDENCE, ANDREW JOHN-
SON NATIONAL MONUMENT, GREENVILLE,
TENNESSEE, 1865. NPS DRAWING. *A restora-
tion data drawing made during the architectural examination. Even though such a record contains numerous notes
of features and conditions observed, such a sheet is only
complete when supplemented by detailed measured draw-*
*ings and photographs. It will be seen that the notes cover
items of work to be done, dates of construction, indications of "original" work, and some "opinions" of the
investigator. Such a drawing is a tool, the information
given will all be confirmed or amended and the final
report and working drawings for the restoration will usually
supercede the "data" drawings.*

When such buildings can be accurately dated, particular notice should be taken of the similarities or differences in their details. Notice both the typical or unusual in methods of construction, floor plans, type of mortar, brick bonds, profiles of moldings, character of carving, pitch of roof, details of chimney caps, types of shingles, and all of the items that, taken together, establish the character of a structure. Of significance, too, are the sizes of framing members and methods of their fabrication, flooring materials, their dimensions and methods of laying; the sort of nails used; the hardware; and glass found in original sash.

A TYPICAL NEW ENGLAND "SALT BOX" HOUSE.

SAN CARLOS MISSION, CARMEL, CALIFORNIA, 1770.

(c) Builders and carpenters handbooks known to have been available to the architect, "undertaker" (as the builder or contractor was often called in the eighteenth century), owner, and all modern published books which are illustrated with photographs and measured drawings showing dated examples of buildings of the period.*

Measured drawings and the record photographs should be made while a superficial examination is being made because the two operations are complementary and should result in a complex and detailed record of the exact appearance of the building at the time the investigation started.

---

*See glossary for an example.

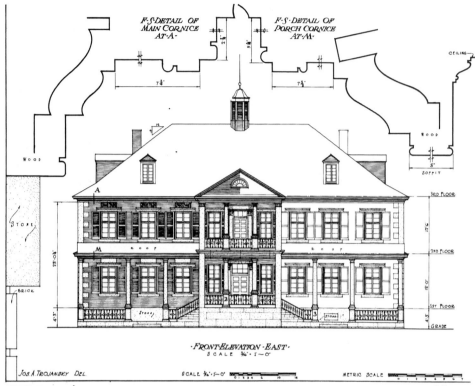

THE KING'S PALACE, ZOAR COMMUNITY, ZOAR, OHIO, EARLY 19TH CENTURY; FRONT ELEVATION EAST. COURTESY OF THE LIBRARY OF CONGRESS. *Historic American Buildings measured drawing—final record drawing.*

It must not be assumed, when taking measurements, that seemingly repetitive features are actually identical or that apparently symmetrical features on a facade are actually so located. All elevations should be completely measured and drawn and cross-sections showing all interior treatment should be made. Scaffolding and surveyor's equipment is often needed.

Large-scale details of all architectural features together with full-size profiles, should be drawn in addition to complete floor plans. Photographic coverage should be exceptionally complete and supplement the work of the draftsman.*

---

*The technique of making measured drawings is fully covered in the *Manual of the Historic American Buildings Survey, Part IX Measured Drawings,* Revised 10/61 compiled by Harley J. McKee and published in draft form by the Eastern Office of the Division of Design and Construction of the National Park Service.

Superficial Examination

A superficial examination should be made of every exposed part of the building, inside and out, excluding no accessible spaces. Facts may be deduced during this examination; also many questions will be raised and clues recorded for later study. It is essential that all features and details observed be described in narrative form where measured drawings fail to record full information. All surface materials, the method of their manufacture or fabrication, utilization in the structure, and relationships one to the other should be noted, dated if possible, and recorded.

This examination of the building should start with a study of its overall form, size, and proportions. Every evidence of change or alteration such as a difference in brickwork (which might be in the brick size, bond, texture, color, or coursing) should be noted. Heads, jambs, and sills of door and window openings in brick structures should be carefully examined for the manner in which the work was finished. It is almost always possible to determine whether or not door and window openings in brick work are in their original locations because it is exceedingly difficult to alter the size of an opening in a brick wall without making the change apparent to even a casual examination.

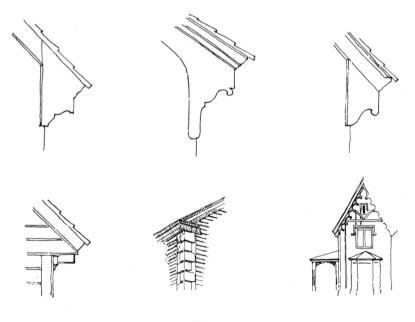

Additional stories are often revealed by changes in the character of brick-work both in walls and around window openings, even though such items as the cornice or trim may appear from a casual examination to have been a part of the original fabric. Frame buildings often show evidences of alterations through changes in the character of the weatherboarding or siding.

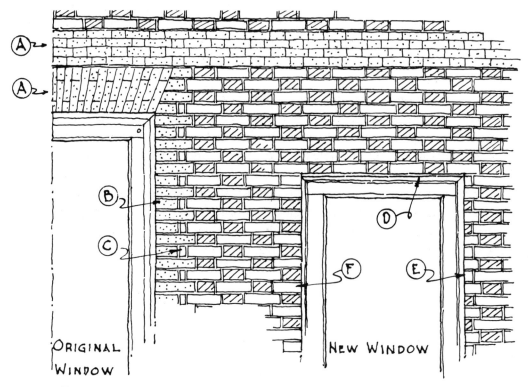

(A) BELT COURSE & JACK ARCH GAGED AND GROUND BRICK.
(B) JAMBS ACCENTED WITH SELECTED SURFACE GROUND BR.
(C) "CLOSURES" START FLEMISH BOND WITH GLAZED HEADERS.
(D) NO JACK ARCH- BRICK CARRIED ON STEEL ANGLE LINTEL.
(E) BRICK CUT TO ACCOMODATE FRAME- BOND NEGLECTED.
(F) FRAME SET ON HEADER JOINT- STRETCHERS CUT.

Clues to window changes (above) and (facing page) basic gambrel roof forms. The proportions, form, and treatment of gable ends of these roofs overlapped less from region to region than many details characteristic of the eighteenth century.

38

The location, form, and detail of dormer windows and the treatment of the roof surfaces should be studied and differences from normal practice recorded. It is unwise to assume that work is or is not a part of the initial construction until investigation provides evidence.

On the other hand, many features and details such as asphalt shingles or imitation brick siding may be generally dated by even the most casual observation; the romantic trim of the Victorian era is not likely to be confused with that of any other period and a heavy muntined small light sash will be recognized at once as earlier than those of the nineteenth century. Such an authentic dateable architectural detail, cannot, of course, be used alone as evidence to date a building. It will be discovered, too, that salvaged material has often been installed in later work.

LONG ISLAND & NEW JERSEY.

The presence or absence of shutters should be noted and each window examined for shutter hardware or evidence of their former presence and if found, record shall be made of its kind or design. It should be noted, too, whether or not the window frames and trim apppear to be a part of the original fabric or later replacements. The glass in the sash should be noted and its thickness and texture, color and imperfections, and even its source or method of manufacture, the nature of the putty, and method of holding the glass in the sash should be recorded. Notice the method of trimming external corners and the openings in wooden houses. Such features have varied through the years, and from place to place, as have the profiles of moldings and the cross sections of weatherboarding.

NEW ENGLAND & S. CAR.

Keep in mind that the purpose of this superficial examination is to note those features which are typical of the period and those which seem to be unusual or different from usual practice. In order to plan the more radical examination which is to follow it is advisable to determine the need for the eventual removal of the parts in question, to decide whether or not any unusual features are an idiosyncrasy of the builder and a part of the original fabric or are actually later additions. There will be many cases where evidence other than that found in this superficial examination will be necessary to be sure of a suspected change or to definitely authenticate an apparently original piece of work.

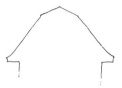

MARYLAND & N. CAROLINA.

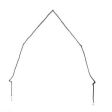

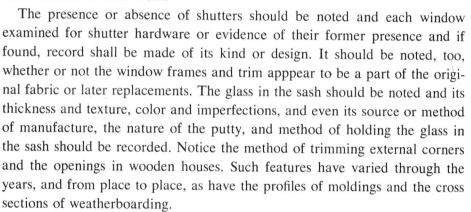

CONN. & N. CAROLINA.

The superficial examination should also include all inside spaces such as attics, cellars, or crawl spaces which may be reached by the examiner without demolishing any part of the structure. The investigation should be made on a space by space basis.

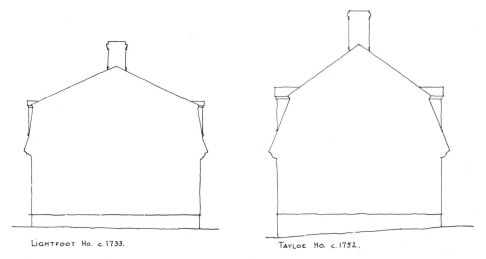

Within a region variations in the same basic gambrel roof form may provide clues to relative dates as may molding profiles. Basic forms vary from decade to decade. Compare pitch and proportion and note the location of dormers. The dormer roof pitch is the same as the roof which receives it.

Alterations, additions, and changes which have occurred during the history of the building are often plainly revealed in the foundation walls. Historical facts supplemented by archaeological dating evidence may be confirmed by the nature of the foundation walls and the character of the superstructure they support. The pavement of basement floors, should be particularly suspect, because brick or stone basement floors, of apparently original construction, have quite often been laid over earlier flooring surfaces.

Particular notice should be taken of the framing of the first floor if it is exposed in the basement; this would include the nature of the structural members, their size, and whether they were fabricated with axes or sawn, and, if the latter, whether with a "pit", band, or circular saw. Fireplaces should be

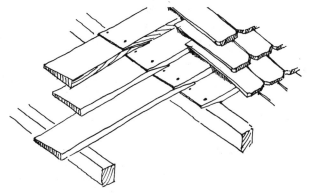

Split siding used as original roof sheathing, later covered with rived shingles found hidden under roofs added later. Both shingles and siding were smoothed, probably with a draw knife. Early split or rived shingles were always smooth, never left with "split" surfaces.

40

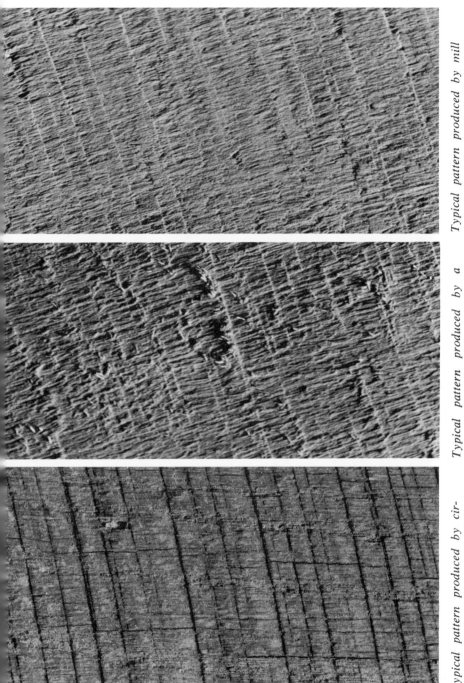

Typical pattern produced by circular saw, dating from the 1850's.

Typical pattern produced by a whip or pit saw, dating from the eighteenth century.

Typical pattern produced by mill or sash saw, dating from the early nineteenth century.

All of the above photos were taken taken at Saratoga Historic National Park, Schuylerville, N. Y. and are NPS photos.

A part of the original frame of Phillip Schuyler's Barn, 1777-1786, in Saratoga National Historic Park, which had been demolished about 1840 and from which some of the material was reused, completely out of original context, in the construction of the Tenant house.

The Tenant house was dismantled in 1963 as a part of the restoration of the group. Henry A. Judd, Supervising Architect for Historic Structures, National Park Service, was able to reassemble enough parts, by identification of notches and joints marked by incised Roman numerals, to reveal not only the arrangement of the members in the original frame but to determine the approximate length of the barn as well.

Architectural research supplemented by historical and archeological evidence may permit an accurate reconstruction of the barn. See also the illustrations of the General Philip Schuyler House on page 59. NPS photo.

given special attention because their design may indicate whether they were used for heating or cooking, thereby revealing the function of the room.

Some basement stories are constructed largely above outside grade and have been used other than as basement rooms. In such cases they may have undergone radical alterations during the course of their history and it will be immediately apparent that a more detailed examination must be made to determine the actual original use of the space.

The study of the overhead floor framing and the masonry walls of the basement, if exposed, must include: a recording of all unusual materials such as steel or metal lintels over window openings; notches for headers cut or built into floor framing members; or mortices which may suggest the location of earlier partition studding, stairwells, or fireplaces.

The examiner must not delude himself that he can remember all he sees as he passes through a building, or indeed, all that he sees during a careful investigation. It is perfectly amazing and frustrating to find, when drawing up field notes in the quiet of the drafting room, that a salient feature observed in the Southeast room has been forgotten. Or was it the Southwest room? On the first floor or second floor? And it seemed so obvious at the time — so obvious that no record was made in the notebook. The examiner should take nothing for granted, particularly his memory, and should devote sufficient time in each space or room to be sure that he overlooks nothing. The crack in the wall, the return of a cornice, the unusual jointing of floor boards, the slight misalignment of paneling, or the notch in a rafter for a collar beam which is not there, may provide the key to the former use and finish of the space.

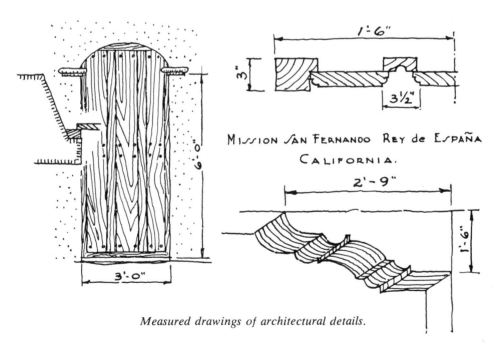

MISSION SAN FERNANDO REY de ESPAÑA
CALIFORNIA.

Measured drawings of architectural details.

43

This superficial examination of the building should also pick out those places where a detailed investigation of painted work should be made. Tentative probing and scraping with a pen knife in protected locations may uncover clues to the former decorative treatment of the building and provide a guide for later investigation with scalpel and magnifying glass, or for later removal of pieces of trim or other parts for a more detailed examination. (Molding profiles, otherwise lost, have been found distinctly traced in paintwork long covered by later trim.)

Buildings with a history through several generations of a prosperous family, may be expected to have been modernized and enlarged a number of times. Mantels will have been changed, fireplaces rebuilt, door and window trim replaced, shutters added or removed, cornices rebuilt to more "modern" designs, roofs raised to permit the addition of whole stories, and many other changes made.

Calvert Vaux, architect in New York in the mid-nineteenth century was concerned, not with preservation and restoration, but with the design of new buildings. He sought through several publications to assist clients to select proper designs for their houses. In his book entitled "Villas and Cottages," (Harper & Brothers 1874) he devotes a chapter to the alteration of an old house in which he wrote, "there are to be found in different parts of the country, many families who have been settled for several generations on the same spot and their old simple wooden homesteads, mended and patched every few years, hold their own with commendable pertinacity. They have no idea of falling to pieces and are altogether too solid and substantial to be pulled down. Now this quality of durability is, of course, in the abstract, an excellent virtue for a house to possess; but it must be confessed that, in such very awkward and ungainly structures as often fall to the lot of these well-settled families, its prevalence could cheerfully be dispensed with, were it not for the many interesting associations and family reminiscences that linger around the old house—." He goes on to say, "it does not often occur that a design can be altered so as to be entirely satisfactory." But one old house he found worthy of modernizing was that of Homer Ramsdell whose family home he "improved" in September of 1855. He says of the work done, "Some of the windows and doors were shifted along a foot or two one way or the other, so as to bring the arrangement of openings into a form that would admit of proper treatment on the exterior . . . . The chief alteration was made by taking a slice off the top of the original stiff old roof, and then bringing up the flat roof of

44

Southeast view before alteration.

Same view after alteration. (both original engravings from "Villas and Cottages," by Calvert Vaux, architect, 1874).

the wing to the new ridge level . . . . Two of the other chimneys, after being taken down as far as was necessary, and tied together with an iron band, were arched over in the garret, and grouped above the ridge into one double stack . . . . the roof was projected all round and fitted with brackets . . . . the verandas were somewhat improved . . ."

Such were the radical changes wrought in one old house at one point in time. The record indicated that there had been previous alterations and no doubt, if the family continued to live in the house or if the house exists today, it has been subjected to further changes. Its history and evolution is typical of the changes which have been made in most of the older buildings that are now candidates for restoration.

Mr. Vaux's "simple wooden homestead" is mentioned both to illustrate the help such a historical document may afford and to point up the sorts of changes frequently made to buildings and which the investigating architect will be called upon to recognize, deduce, and understand from his study of the fabric of the building itself.

LYONS - JONES HOUSE, ROCHESTER, INDIANA, ARCHITECT UN- 1856. *Restorationists must stand in awe and not in judgment of the manisfestations of the taste of past generations..*

ST. CHARLES, MON-
TANA, ARCHITECT
UNKNOWN, C. 1840.

*This far western example
was not unlike many east-
ern business blocks.*

In practice it will be found that very few buildings older than a single generation are still in their original condition and there are even fewer for which there is documentation, even in most general terms of the changes made by various owners and occupants. This regrettable lack of corroborative documentary evidence makes exhaustive study of a building absolutely essential if the final result is to be an authentic restoration.

Dateable hardware, paneling, fireplace treatments, rough wavy plaster, inlaid flooring, gas lamps, worn stair treads, wood shingles, deeply weathered brickwork, or badly eroded masonry, even molding profiles identical to dated examples or obviously "antique" glass must not be accepted as prima facie evidence of any particular date or period. The examination in depth which is the next step, will seek to confirm the dates on sequences of installation or construction of every part of the building. In any event, many facts, questions, and hunches will emerge from the superficial examination. The investigator is well-advised to refrain from jumping to final or specific conclusions until he has completed a detailed examination of the entire structure.

The procedure outlined thus far may be applied to any restoration project, but from this point on the work is more influenced by the particular project under consideration. In the words of the late Mr. S. P. Moorhead F.A.I.A. of Colonial Williamsburg, "The basic controls of a restoration project are date, culture, geography, climate, and proposed scope."

So far as the architectural research is concerned, the most important controls are perhaps that of the restoration date and proposed use decided upon. Once these have been fixed, then the extent of architectural research necessary can be established.

In this next phase of the work a complete and detailed investigation inevitably results in the destruction or at least the removal of work of past genera-

18th century.

47

THE CONCEPTION MISSION, SAN ANTONIO, TEXAS, MISSIONARY FATHER MARGIL, C. 1731.

HOUSE IN VIRGINIA CITY, NEVADA, C1860.

HOUSES IN OTWELL, MARYLAND.

48

A BUILDING IN FREDERICKSBURG, VIRGINIA, C. 1730. *Essentially unchanged through many generations, individual buildings and street fronts have withstood the onslaught of progress and continue to serve with grace and dignity. Facing page, top and center, some remain unchanged while (bottom) others have grown through the years.*

tions. Even though many original parts may eventually be returned to their former places, the operation is inevitably less convincing than the restoration of the original work left in place.

Detailed Examination

Having assimilated all that is known about the property from documentary and historical references, studied the findings of the archaeologist, made measured drawings and an examination of every accessible part of the structure, taken photographs, determined the tentative date for restoration and established the basic presentation or use program, it now becomes necessary to probe into the fabric of the structure itself. This operation is necessary to determine accurately the form, character, and sequence of the various alterations, additions and changes to which the structure has been subject during the course of its history.

49

On the other hand, the extent of the investigation may be limited by its importance to the proposed use and interpretation. There will be little need to determine the exact nature and form of a structure in, say, 1780 if the period to which it is to be restored is 1820 and the "investigation" would involve removal and subsequent replacement of authentic work of 1820.

That probing which must be done should be conducted with care, understanding, and a delicate loving touch; it must be remembered that this is not a demolition project to be handled by swinging a ball and snapping a bucket.

Many parts that are removed may be replaced during the restoration if they can be authenticated as of the period to which the building is to be restored. No apparently original part or member should be removed even though its condition is such that it must be replaced, until it has been studied *in situ* and photographed for future reference.* All parts which are removed must be permanently identified, marked, and keyed to drawings recording their original location. Chalk or pencil is inadequate for this purpose because very often

*Of particular pertinence is "Maintenance of Restored Buildings" by Henry A. Judd, *Building Research* Sept.-Oct. 1964.

VIEUX CARRE, NEW ORLEANS, LOUISIANA. *The charm of light and shade and scale graced with the patina of age cannot be reproduced in convincing form.*

considerable time elapses between the removal of features and the reconstruction of the building. During this period they may be moved or subjected to inclement weather. Die-stamped copper tags permanently affixed to the back of each member, while expensive, may prove worth the cost.

Even though the sponsor and the historians will have agreed upon the particular time in history to which the building should be restored, possibly even before having embarked upon the restoration project, no part should be arbitrarily cast aside and destroyed until all of the evidence has been collected and evaluated by the examining architects.

The reason for the preservation of the building should be clearly understood by all persons on the project in order to avoid the careless loss or damage to any of its parts. In almost every instance, no matter what the intended use of the restored building, its preservation as a part of our architectural heritage is of paramount importance. In some manner and to some degree its architectural history will be made available to visitors in a visual as well as an auditory presentation. Therefore, the fabric of the building should be as authentic and accurate as humanly possible. This means that the purpose of the restoration is not to make a new building out of an old one, but to preserve, for an indeterminate period, the actual physical manifestations of the imagination and craftsmanship of its builders.

Procedure

Whether the examination of the structure should start at the basement, the attic, or the exterior is a matter of individual determination and inclination. The architect, through his study of the documents and of the building, should be aware of those portions which are suspect or which, if investigated further, may be expected either to yield more clues and answer niggling problems, or to create further enigmas. No matter where the investigation starts, each step should be calculated to destroy as little as possible of the building. It would, of course, be ideal if all of the architectural history could be learned or verified without removing any part of the building, but this is rarely feasible.

In this operation of "removal to look behind" a detailed knowledge of materials and their uses in the area is of the utmost importance. For example, "Masonite," wall board, plaster board, or "Gyplap" are obviously not materials used in the eighteenth century and their presence under or behind a wain-

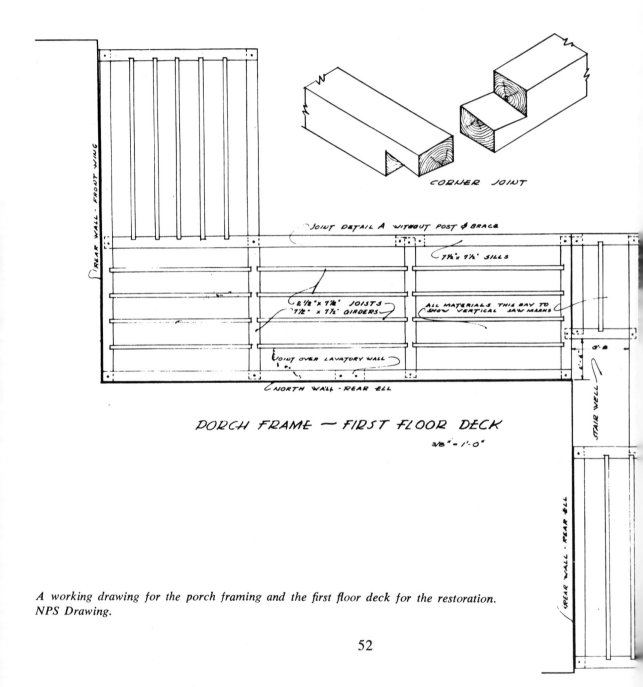

CORNER JOINT

JOINT DETAIL A WITHOUT POST & BRACE

7½" x 7½" SILLS

REAR WALL - FRONT WING

2½" x 7½" JOISTS
7½" x 7½" GIRDERS

ALL MATERIALS THIS BAY TO SHOW VERTICAL SAW MARKS

JOINT OVER LAVATORY WALL

NORTH WALL - REAR ELL

STAIR WELL

REAR WALL - REAR ELL

PORCH FRAME — FIRST FLOOR DECK

3/8" = 1'-0"

A working drawing for the porch framing and the first floor deck for the restoration. NPS Drawing.

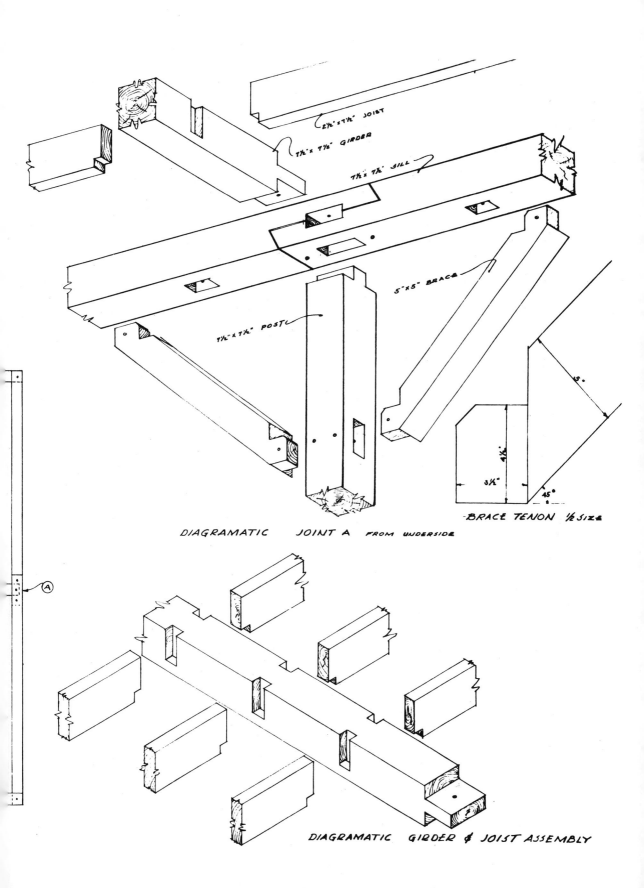

2½" x 7½" JOIST

7½" x 7½" GIRDER

7½" x 7½" SILL

5" x 5" BRACE

7½" x 7½" POST

DIAGRAMATIC JOINT A FROM UNDERSIDE

BRACE TENON ½ SIZE

5"

4½"

3½"

45°

(A)

DIAGRAMATIC GIRDER & JOIST ASSEMBLY

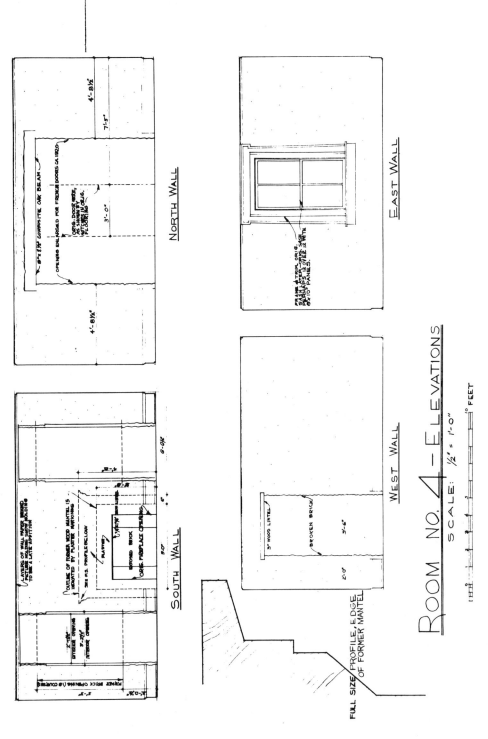

ROOM NO. 4—ELEVATIONS

SCALE: ½" = 1'-0"

NORTH WALL

EAST WALL

SOUTH WALL

WEST WALL

ANDREW JOHNSON RESIDENCE, ANDREW JOHNSON NATIONAL MONUMENT, GREENVILLE, TENN. NPS DRAWING.

Restored data drawing recording features discovered in the architectural examination. Sketches of this kind should be supplemented by photographs such as these shown on the facing page.

54

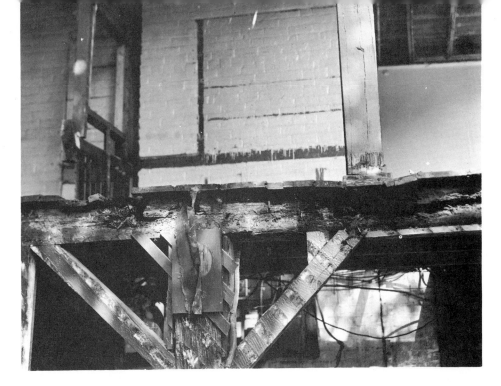

Above, the framing of the original porch on the right, the addition of about 1869, and the patch in the original sill made in the early 1900's are recorded in this record photograph taken during the architectural examination. See the drawing on pages 52 and 53. Below, the typical condition of the porch framing. Even though the work was so badly deteriorated it had to be replaced, enough evidence remained to permit an accurate replacement. NPS Photos.

scoting identified as the work of the brothers Adam might be taken as positive evidence that the paneling was not in an original location.

Baseboards, sections of flooring, plaster, lathing, or any part or member recognized as twentieth century (unless, of course, the building is known to have been built in the twentieth century) can be removed without serious

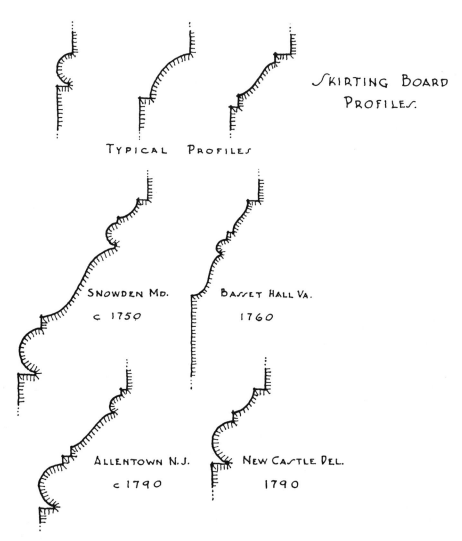

SKIRTING BOARD PROFILES.

TYPICAL PROFILES

SNOWDEN MD.
c 1750

BASSET HALL VA.
1760

ALLENTOWN N.J.
c 1790

NEW CASTLE DEL.
1790

The character of moldings change from period to period and, though less often, from region to region. Earlier moldings closely followed the pattern books based upon classical antiquity whereas nineteenth century designers expressed a fondness for deep undercutting and a proliferation of members.

56

architectural damage and expose structural features which provide dating evidence. (Only study and experience will guide the architect who might be inclined to suspect that the flooring *per se* is modern.)

Floorboards provide the same relative dating evidence as any other wooden member: the saw and plane marks, means of sizing, treatment of the

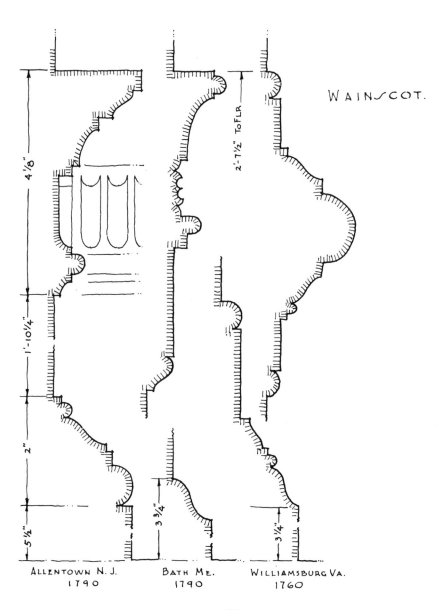

WAINSCOT.

ALLENTOWN N. J.
1790

BATH ME.
1790

WILLIAMSBURG VA.
1760

57

under or back surface, and method of laying, as well as the nails (often multiple sets of nail holes reveal the existence of earlier flooring) used to secure them, all provide clues as to the dates of fabrication and installation.

Exposed joists will reveal a similar story. If the portion of flooring selected for removal were bounded by a row of end butt joints, then the flooring may have been added over a former framed hole in the floor construction, possibly for a stairway or a trap door, the passage of a chimney, or some other reason.

ORIGINAL LATER
BASE.

Baseboards, if removed, will reveal, in addition to the nature of the board itself, the methods of application; if these trade practices of the area are understood, they will indicate the approximate date of installation. For example, in many eighteenth century frame houses baseboards were placed directly against the studding and plaster work was brought down on top of them. It is thus important to know at what date or approximate date the practice of carrying plaster work down or near to the floor and applying the baseboards on top of the plaster came into common usage.

Paneling and trim, when removed, will expose more of the framing of the wall, the members of which should be studied for evidence of their manufacture, fabrication, and application: whether held in place by nails, or mortised, tennoned, and pegged, or a combination of the two. Look also for evidence of re-use or former connections. Again, local trade practices throughout the years should be understood.

Plaster work, if obviously modern or hopelessly deteriorated should be removed to expose the laths which in turn should be removed, bit by bit, if it shows evidence of modern manufacture and installation. Wholesale removal of plaster work is not recommended because of the danger of destroying evidence which will be invaluable at a later date. The structural frame of the building will provide mute evidence to the initiated of the possible date of its fabrication and erection and, because of the probable existence of headers, notches, mortises, molded or chamfered corners, may indicate the previous location of doors, windows, or openings.

Framing members, whether inside or out, structural or furring, frequently reveal, through the existence of nail holes, a former application of the covering of an earlier period. An early eighteenth century brick building, formerly a store or a shop, was restored in the twentieth century with plaster walls. The architectural examiners thought that the plaster work which had been applied

Above, a contrast in trade practices.

GENERAL PHILIP SCHUYLER HOUSE, WEST WALL OF THE DINING ROOM, SARATOGA NATIONAL HISTORIC PARK, SCHUYLERVILLE, NEW YORK. NPS PHOTO. *Above, research establishing the dates of locally available materials is essential. Saw lath made by Philip Schuyler in his own saw mills was used on this wall in 1777, the doorway was closed with accordian-split lath about 1830. Below, the height of the original mantel is indicated in this photograph of the fireplace wall in the parlor by the termination of the plaster. Wallpaper with wheat-sheaf pattern apparently was the first applied, in the 1790's. Eight layers of paper had been hung over the first one on the back of which an English tax stamp was found.*

directly to the brick was original. Many years later a further investigation revealed that regularly spaced vertical wooden nailing strips buried in the masonry walls had been covered by the plaster work. The original use for the nailing strips was to support horizontal boarding or paneling. This treatment was indicated by the nail holes spaced at regular intervals in the nailing strips.

Nail holes, wherever found, may be of tremendous importance. All exposed members should be carefully examined for them since they indicate the nature of the work which might have been applied in previous periods. For example, a long abandoned stairway location may be suggested by the floor framing. The location and nature of nail holes found in studding along the wall may lead to the discovery of the actual slope, run and location of the stair. It would be well in such an investigation also to make an effort to find

INDEPENDENCE HALL, PHILADELPHIA, PENNSYLVANIA. NPS PHOTO. *This is a key photograph made of the north wall of the assembly room during the architectural examination. Significant features have been outlined in white. Restoration work was in progress when this picture was taken; attention is called to the strengthening of the floor above the addition of new floor joists and steel beams.*

60

In the photograph (right) of the center window in the north wall of the assembly room it will be seen that the bricks, formerly covered by architraves and splayed jamb paneling, are clean and show no traces of plaster. In the detail photograph (to the left) at the right hand jamb, is evidence of the architraves. Arrow No. 1 points to the wrought iron anchor (bent over in 1816) with offset flange which abutted the vertical architrave. A handwrought nail through this flange would have secured the architrave in the masonry. Arrow No. 2 indicates traces of red-oxide and gray paint which resulted from prime-painting the woodwork prior to plastering. Note the clean bricks behind the architrave, and the plaster evidence to the right of this vertical line. The plaster was removed in 1816, pilasters were installed (thus covering and hence preserving the original evidence), and the walls plastered. The 1816 plaster was removed in 1831. Arrow No. 3 points to the edge of the window opening.

the evidence of the former existence of newel posts in the floor construction at both the bottom and the top of the suspected stairway location.

Old materials have always held a fascination for owners and builders. Often paneling, mantels, or architectural trim has been re-used, in some cases entire buildings have been built of salvaged materials from a period near enough to that of the original building date to be confusing. The installation of such salvaged material by able craftsmen over other old work very often complicates identification for the examiner. (The degree of difficulty may be assessed when it is remembered that Independence Hall in Philadelphia has been "restored" several times!)

Architectural woodwork such as door and window trim, fireplace mantels, over-mantels and paneling are particularly subject to change and alteration as each succeeding generation seeks to modernize. The architectural investigator

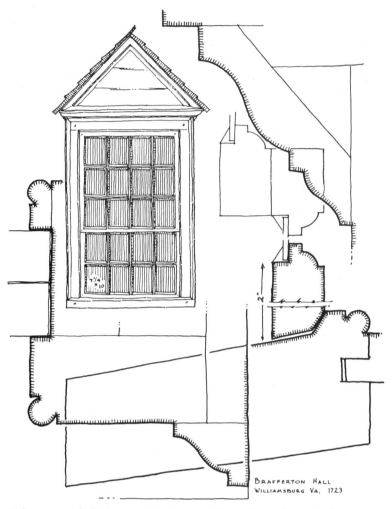

BRAFFERTON HALL
WILLIAMSBURG VA. 1723

Dormer windows reveal distinct regional as well as chronological characteristics in design and construction. The details of the sash on the other hand, conform more closely to chronological sequence.

must satisfy himself that every apparently original bit of architectural wood-work is indeed a part of the initial construction and, if not, determine when it was installed. Architectural trim should be handled with exceptional care even though it may not be of the original structure. There are occasions when old unoriginal work is to be preferred to replacements in a restored room, especially when authentic members from a later period remain and the detailing for the period of the original work must be conjectural.

Exterior features such as porches, dormer windows, sash, and roof coverings are especially subject to alterations because their very rapid deterioration

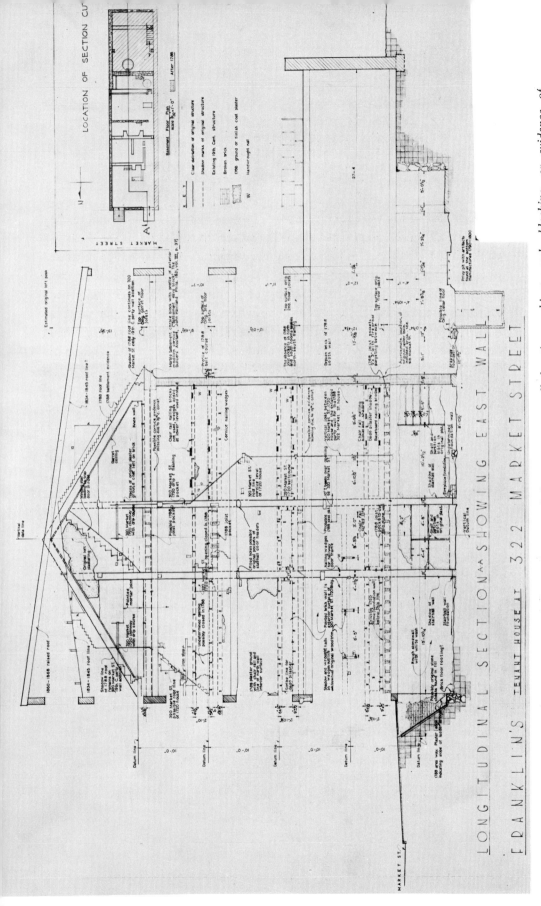

LONGITUDINAL SECTION SHOWING EAST WALL

FRANKLIN'S TENANT HOUSE AT 322 MARKET STREET

Record drawing showing longitudinal section and the east wall. All changes and additions are shown and dated. Significant features such as joist holes, traces of former wall location, cabinet work, blocking, or evidence of architectural trim, remaining original plaster, and the like are clearly indicated. See photo following page.

makes frequent replacement necessary. They so obviously reflect the changing appreciation of what makes good taste in architecture because, when renewed, their design is often brought up-to-date.

Dating the Sections

The establishment of the relative dates of entire portions of a structure may be somewhat more complicated than that of features because in some cases a whole building has been moved in one piece from its original site to be added to another building as a wing or an ell. When the connection between these two differently dated wings is exposed, the architectural examiner may need the archaeological evidence to determine which was the first on the site even though he may be able to identify the relative age of the two sections from their intrinsic evidence. Wings, ells, or porches added to houses are frequently

HOUSE AT 322 MARKET STREET, KNOWN AS THE BENJAMIN FRANKLIN TENANT HOUSE, PHILADELPHIA, PENNSYLVANIA, 1786. NPS PHOTO. *The east wall of the cellar kitchen with modern additions, plaster and whitewash removed. The original plaster remains revealing not only the layers of paint, applied over the years, but the locations of the shelf and end boards of the original kitchen dresser or cupboard. See also the longitudinal section showing the east wall on the drawing (previous page).*

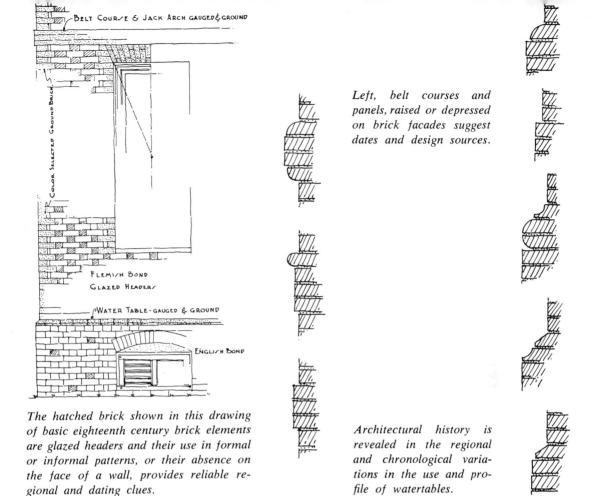

Left, belt courses and panels, raised or depressed on brick facades suggest dates and design sources.

The hatched brick shown in this drawing of basic eighteenth century brick elements are glazed headers and their use in formal or informal patterns, or their absence on the face of a wall, provides reliable regional and dating clues.

Architectural history is revealed in the regional and chronological variations in the use and profile of watertables.

documented. This investigation should commence with an exposure of their connections to other parts of the house. As each feature or part is removed, the structure revealed should be carefully studied, measured, drawn, and photographed for the record.*

The removal of parts and study of the structure should continue until the period of each unit of construction has been established. The notes and photographs taken during the course of the investigation should provide the necessary information for drawing plans, elevations, and sections of the several periods of construction dated by the intrinsic evidence in the structure itself, by historical evidence, by archaeological finds, or by a combination of the three.

The following features should be given special study:

Brick work: brick size, method of manufacture, color; texture; bond; char-

---

*See "Photographic Records in Restoration" by Jack E. Boucher, Appendix.

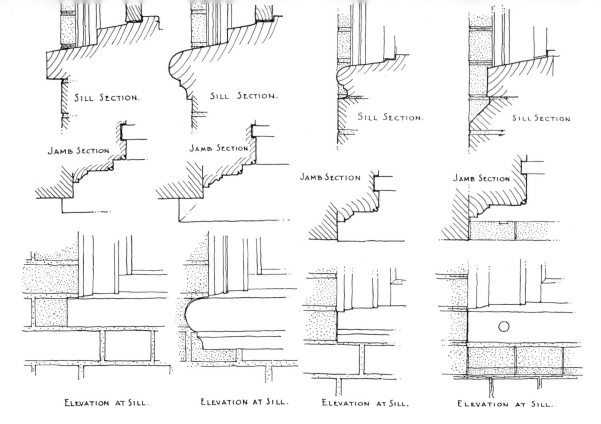

SILL SECTION. SILL SECTION. SILL SECTION. SILL SECTION

JAMB SECTION JAMB SECTION JAMB SECTION JAMB SECTION

ELEVATION AT SILL. ELEVATION AT SILL. ELEVATION AT SILL. ELEVATION AT SILL.

The design and construction of window frames reveals date of fabrication and cultural background of the designer and builder.

The more elaborate molded sills are usually earlier than the simpler sort.

acter of profile of jointing; pointing; composition and color of mortar; treatment of jambs; heads and sills of openings; use of brick uniform in color around openings, for water table or belt courses; the use of "surface ground" brick, gauged brick, molded or carved brick; inset panels in rubbed or gauged brick or plaster; the absence or presence of water tables and/or belt courses and their form; the use of flat jack arches, segmental arches, round arches; the form and detail of the construction of chimney stacks and caps; the formation of weatherings or haunches on chimneys; and the overall workmanship of masonry work.

Exterior Wall Covering: clapboards, split or rived, band sawn, circular sawn or planed, tapered or rectangular in section, molded or un-molded; use of trim at external and internal corners; treatment of window and door openings, method of placement on the wall, whether with beveled or rabbeted weatherings or with through (square) joints between the boards; the use of architectural trim such as pilasters at corners, belt or

66

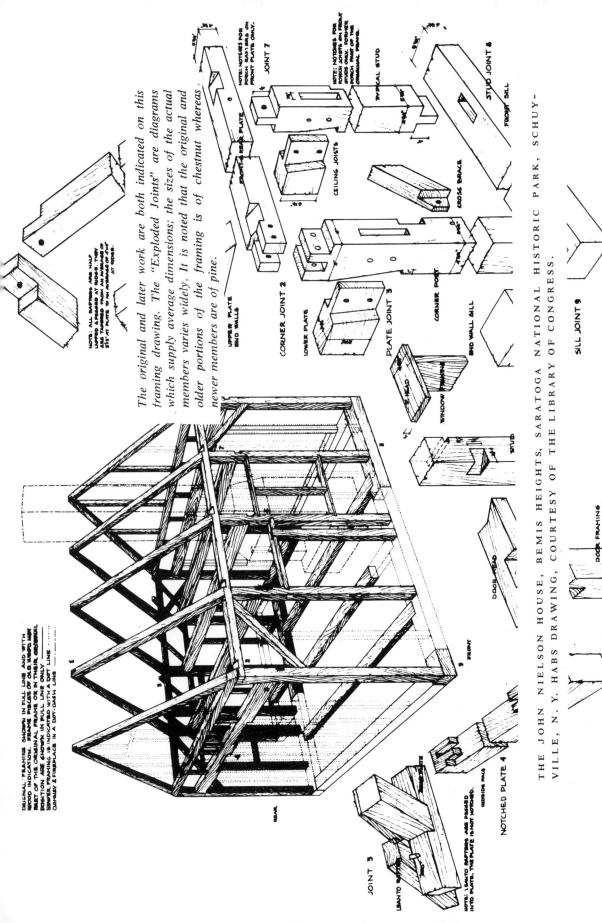

The original and later work are both indicated on this framing drawing. The "Exploded Joints" are diagrams which supply average dimensions; the sizes of the actual members varies widely. It is noted that the original and older portions of the framing is of chestnut whereas newer members are of pine.

THE JOHN NIELSON HOUSE, BEMIS HEIGHTS, SARATOGA NATIONAL HISTORIC PARK, SCHUY-
VILLE, N. Y. HABS DRAWING, COURTESY OF THE LIBRARY OF CONGRESS.

EXPLODED JOINTS

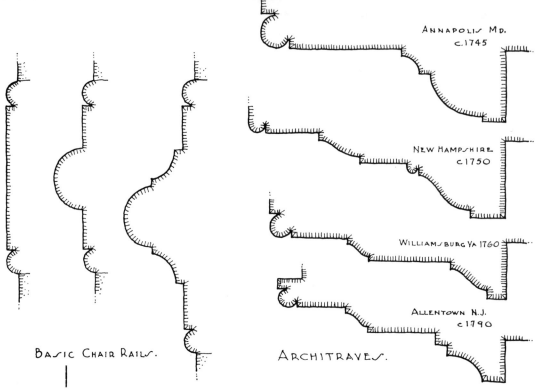

ANNAPOLIS MD.
c.1745

NEW HAMPSHIRE
c.1750

WILLIAMSBURG VA 1760

ALLENTOWN N.J.
c.1790

BASIC CHAIR RAILS.

ARCHITRAVES.

Left, forms widely used in many regions with but minor variations in scale and profile. Right, the popularity of the pattern book during the eighteenth century resulted in a strong resemblance in the work done in several regions, significant variations appear mostly in the use of carving rather than in molding profiles. Measured drawings by the author.

water table courses and cornices; and the method of covering the cheeks or sides of dormer windows.

Roof Coverings: wooden shingles, dimension and design, split, rived or sawn; tile or slate or evidence of their previous application; split or rived clapboards; tile or stone; old thatch, and the form of the roof itself.

Species of Wood: degree of consistency of use for various purposes. (Regional and chronological variations will be found.)

Framing Members: their size and proportion; method of fabrication axe, adze, or sawing, and if the last, what type of sawing; methods of jointing; structural system employed; existence of molded corners, chamfers, or lambs tongues; use of sill girts, summer beams, headers, attic collar beams, ridge poles, and their dual uses as door frames and trim.

Floor Boards: Sizes and methods of fabrication (sized four sides or sized three sides and fitted to bearings by foot adzing); method of jointing—butt, tongue and groove, or splined; face, blind nailed, or pegged; and whether installed before or after the interior partitions were erected (the use of double flooring was rare in any but the most elegant buildings before the nineteenth century).

Lath: Dimension and method of fabrication, method of breaking joints.

Architectural Trim: Character, profile of moldings, methods of application, formation of joints both external and internal.

Moldings: Dated sequences of changing profiles for similar members will provide identification of relative periods; muntin thicknesses and profiles are particularly easy to spot; profiles of door and window architraves; moldings on doors and interior paneling; crown molds and other members of cornices; size and location of corner-beads are revealing; and the relationship of profiles, one to another, in the composition of base or skirting boards, chair rails, architraves and cornices, hand rails, balusters and stair brackets; and the tell-tale marks of the tools used in their fabrication.

Painted Work: Remnants of paint found in protected locations after the earlier removal of trim or other member or the subsequent covering by later work will provide relative dating and design evidence. The dentil found at Independence Hall, shown in the photograph herewith, points up graphically how even the smallest scrap can provide invaluable clues.

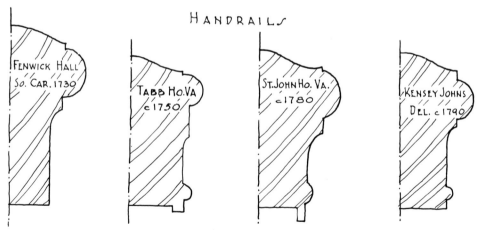

HANDRAILS

Hand rails went through a period of simplification in the early eighteenth century to be followed by a period of even greater elaboration of size and profile in the 1890's. Measured drawing by the author.

69

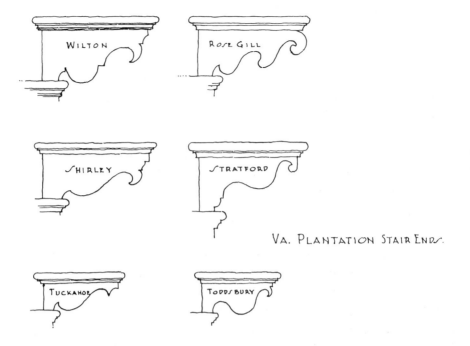

WILTON

ROSE GILL

SHIRLEY

STRATFORD

VA. PLANTATION STAIR ENDS.

TUCKAHOE

TODDSBURY

Basic forms of stair brackets were much the same throughout the colonial period and later variations through the use of carving and scroll saw cut-outs provide the opportunity to identify regional characteristics. Examples from other areas are shown on page 72.

Sequences established by the careful removal, layer by layer, exposing a sample of each coat from the naked wood out to the one most recently applied should be made.* This will provide dating evidence only when historical research can document repainting or use of specific colors or when colors have been covered by dateable architectural features, but it will help when related to dated examples of the availability and use of certain colors. The investigation is essential to the accurate selection of the colors which were formerly used in the house. A study of painted work applies, of course, both to the exterior and the interior.

Record of Colors Used: It is important that samples of each paint color used in the restoration be mixed and kept. The samples may be wet, dry, or

---

*The difficulty in determining the original or first color may be assessed when it is found that local trade practices of the period sometimes called for up to ten coats of paint to decorate a wall. There were times too when to make our task more difficult the original builders used colored plaster which provided the finish for a number of years before any paint at all was applied. See Glossary, *Painting.*

INDEPENDENCE HALL, PHILADELPHIA, PENNSYLVANIA, 1732-1740.
NPS PHOTO. *Wooden dentil found wedged between the brick wall and the original floor joist in the center niche of the east wall of the assembly room. This area was covered by a surviving section of floor boards laid in 1816. The dentil is the only known remnant of the original cornice which was removed in the alterations of 1816. This attribution is based upon the sequence of paint layering which is similar to that found on the original cockleshell frieze. The significance of this dentil can hardly be overestimated. When used in conjunction with the paint traces of the "swell'd" frieze and architrave, the entire entablature can be established with reasonable certainty. The height of the dentil also establishes the proportions of the cornice. The dentil is shown in its normal position (the top inside corner is broken off). It measures 1 - 5/16" deep by 2" high.*

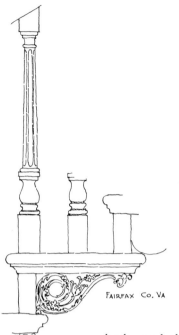

Stair brackets from various areas. Compare these with the ones from Virginia plantations shown on page 70.

both, and their composition or formula should be noted.* The sample tables should also record the exact location of the paint to which the sample was matched, whether in the building being restored or in another.

It is presumed that the colors used in the restoration will be taken from paint samples discovered in the course of architectural examination of the building and that they will therefore be authentic. Samples are important historical records as well as guides to painters doing maintenance painting. Paint, unfortunately, is inclined to change color or hue with the years, particularly if exposed to sunlight or the elements. The making and preservation of wet and dry samples or some other permanent record is therefore of primary importance. The establishment of a marking and identification system for samples is essential and the importance of cross referencing, in case for any reason the system is changed, cannot be over emphasized.

A beautiful color used in restoration work is less significant if its identification with a building is lost. The author recalls a vast set of paint samples collected from various dated examples over a wide area for use as documents in a major period restoration project; they lost their scientific usefulness when they were renumbered by an ambitious painting superintendent who failed to record the locations of the original work from which they were copied.

---

*See also, "Painting and Finishing Research Tools" by Penelope Hartshorne. *Building Research* Sept.-Oct., 1964.

Nails: their size, form, design, method of fabrication, application, and use; also the negative evidence of nails, the holes left in woodwork after they have been withdrawn provide excellent clues. This is true in spite of the fact that in early times nails were difficult to come by and, like woodwork, were often re-used; great care is necessary in determining whether the location of a particular nail is an original one or a secondary one.

Hardware: design, manufacture, materials, method of application, use, size, shape and location of holes for nails or screws.

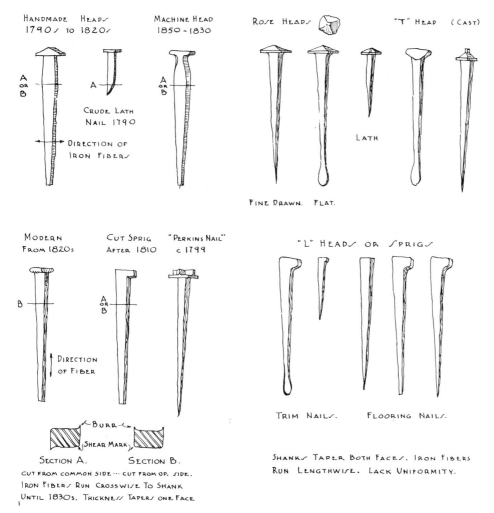

HANDMADE HEADS 1790s TO 1820s

MACHINE HEAD 1850–1830

ROSE HEADS

"T" HEAD (CAST)

A OR B

A

CRUDE LATH NAIL 1790

A OR B

DIRECTION OF IRON FIBERS

LATH

FINE DRAWN. FLAT.

MODERN FROM 1820s

CUT SPRIG AFTER 1810

"PERKINS NAIL" c 1799

"L" HEADS OR SPRIGS

B

A OR B

DIRECTION OF FIBER

TRIM NAILS.   FLOORING NAILS.

BURR

SHEAR MARK

SECTION A.   SECTION B.

CUT FROM COMMON SIDE ··· CUT FROM OP. SIDE.
IRON FIBERS RUN CROSSWISE TO SHANK
UNTIL 1830s. THICKNESS TAPERS ONE FACE

SHANKS TAPER BOTH FACES. IRON FIBERS
RUN LENGTHWISE. LACK UNIFORMITY.

Left, machine cut nails from 1790. Right, Hand-wrought nails — 17th, 18th, and 19th centuries.

73

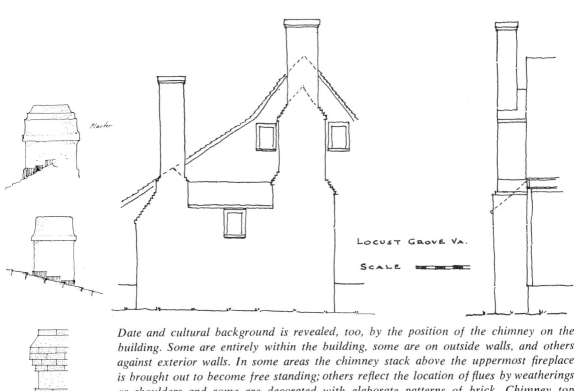

Plaster

LOCUST GROVE VA.

SCALE

Date and cultural background is revealed, too, by the position of the chimney on the building. Some are entirely within the building, some are on outside walls, and others against exterior walls. In some areas the chimney stack above the uppermost fireplace is brought out to become free standing; others reflect the location of flues by weatherings or shoulders and some are decorated with elaborate patterns of brick. Chimney top forms, too, vary from region to region and in some areas may have examples which provide dating evidence.

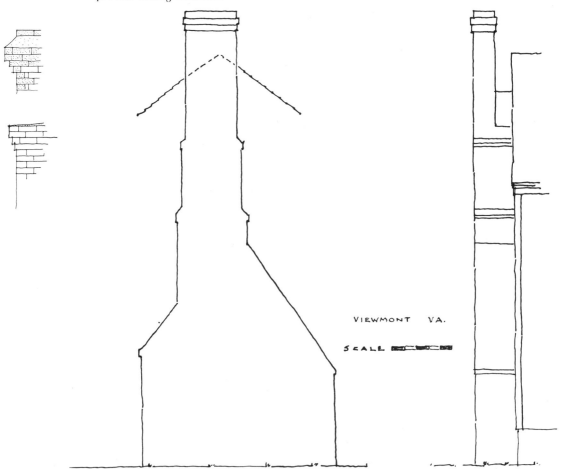

VIEWMONT VA.

SCALE

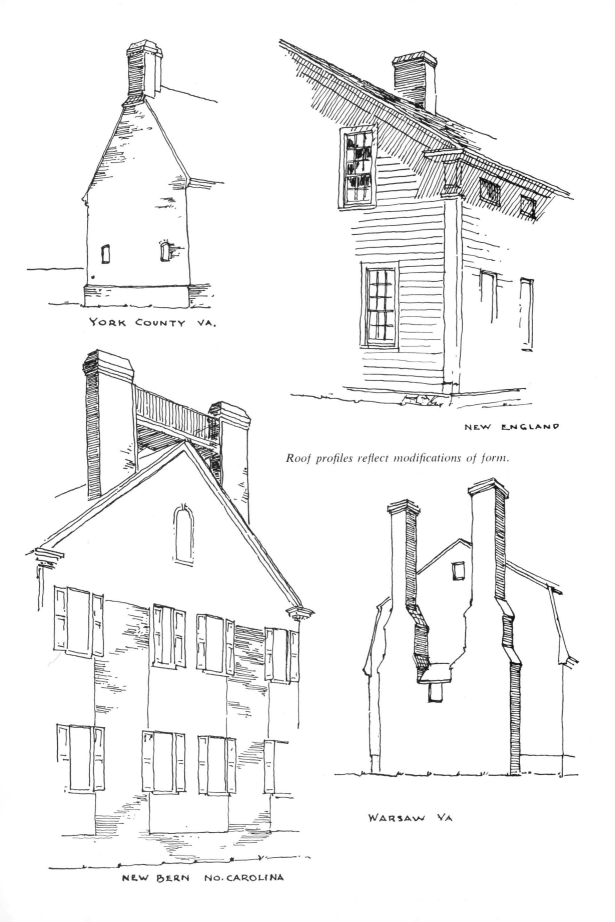

YORK COUNTY VA.

NEW ENGLAND

Roof profiles reflect modifications of form.

NEW BERN NO. CAROLINA

WARSAW VA

VIRGINIA CITY, MONTANA, C. 1865. *Rude, commonplace, and usual build-*
ings reveal a way of life as clearly as the more sophisticated. Touches of architectural
woodwork from earlier times and other places are wrought into the fabric of utilitarian
structures. Regrettably, such buildings are the first to go because they are not
appreciated as any kind of art until they have practically all been replaced. Some of the
evidence offered of life in the nineteenth century, directly related to that of the
eighteenth, still exists and is worth preservation.

76

The use of hardware of improper design is one of the more usual errors in restorations. Few details in a building more clearly reflect changes in technology and design taste and none has been more often neglected. The hardware on doors, windows, shutters, cabinets, and the like are all directly related to the design of architectural members. Surface mounted, offset, or mortised items cannot often be used interchangeably and even if the part is gone the ghosted evidence of its former application may often be found. Conversely, if a piece of hardware is not to be found in a position where it is normally used, the originality of the architectural work may be suspect.

Glass or Glazing: the method of manufacture, crown, plate, or rolled; its color and the number and character of the imperfections such as pebbles, bubbles, wrinkles or other deficiencies, its thickness and variations in thickness; the size of the lights and their number and disposition, six over six, six over nine, etc.

1723

1750

Miscellaneous Features that will provide dating evidence if their local use can be proven by documented examples include: Stone work, type used, surface treatment, bond, profile of joints, material composition of pointing mortar, back up mortar. Brickwork, size, clay composition, surface texture or character, method of forming, type of kiln and firing material used for burning, bonds used, width of joints, character of pointing, offsets and weatherings, chimney and parapet caps, use of nailing blocks, use of gauged brick, surface ground brick, type of mortar. Roof pitch and covering, system of laying re-entrant roof angles or valleys, weathering adjacent to vertical walls or dormers, design and proportion of former windows. Basic design treatment of the facades, the windows, cornices, doorways, gable ends. Use of metal for grills, shutter hardware, flashings, rain water conductors. Interior architectural finish including doors, windows, trim, chair rails, wainscoting, stairways, cornices in wood or plaster, ceiling decoration, painting and wall papers.

1760

1790

In the study of more recent work worthy of preservation or restoration do not overlook: Methods of heating—room heaters, of brick, tile, cast iron or steel designed for burning coal, of gas, oil or electricity. Lighting systems—lamps, gas (buried and long forgotten piping), electric direct and indirect current. Food preparation and serving, notice devices used, their location, fuel burned. Dumb-waiters. Bell systems for intercommunication between parts of the house. Sanitary and other plumbing systems.

1780

Muntin width provides dating evidence.

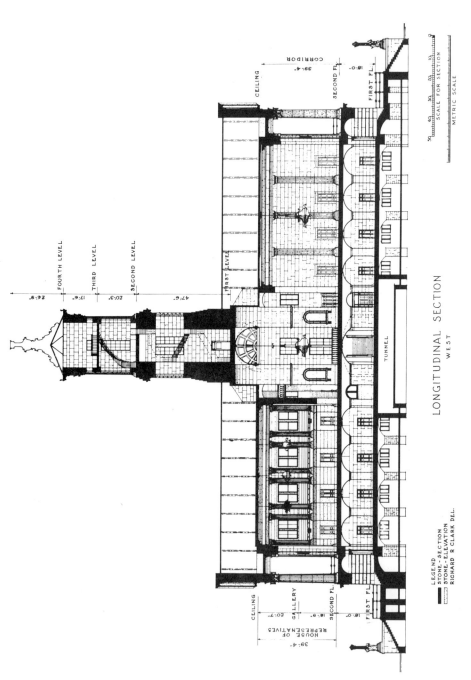

LONGITUDINAL SECTION
WEST

THE TENNESSEE STATE CAPITOL, NASHVILLE, TENNESSEE, WILLIAM STRICKLAND, ARCHITECT, 1945-1949, HABS DRAWING, COURTESY OF THE LIBRARY OF CONGRESS.

This is a survey measured drawing — final record draw-ing of the longitudinal section and forms the basis for the working drawings. Additions may be made to show the new work required or the drawing may be supplemented by additional drawings depending upon the scope of the work required.

EXECUTION OF
A RESTORATION

Like all other construction projects, a restoration is guided by working drawings and specifications. These should indicate adequately the scope and detail of all of the work to be done, materials required, and methods of application.

The specific and detailed resolution of the problems outlined in the previous chapters will provide the architect with the program for the project. In addition to the space requirements of the proposed use, the nature of that use will indicate the mechanical equipment which will be required in the structure and, where historical authenticity is desired, will define the latitude the designer will be allowed in the selection and installation of such equipment. For example, in most cases it is not essential to preserve the historic integrity of structural framing, although care should be taken to avoid excessive elimination of the sags and settlements of age. The structure must, of course, be stabilized and made sound, but the signs of age are lost if it is made plumb and level in every part. It is essential, however, that finished spaces, both inside and out are not marred by the obvious presence of such essential services as heating, air conditioning, electrical equipment, fire alarms, telephones, etc.

Working Drawings

Working drawings for a restoration project should be accurately drawn to scale and figured dimensions should agree with scaled dimensions. Restoration drawings differ from those for a new structure in that those for the resto-

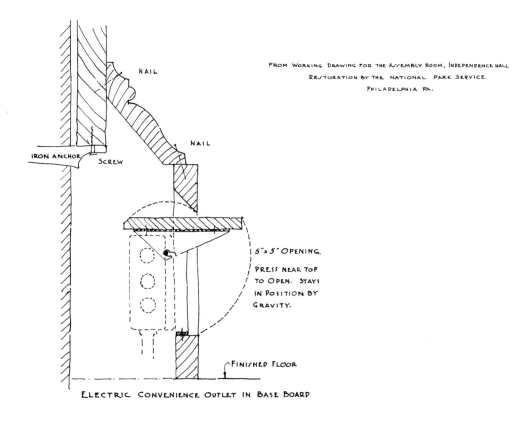

FROM WORKING DRAWING FOR THE ASSEMBLY ROOM, INDEPENDENCE HALL
RESTORATION BY THE NATIONAL PARK SERVICE
PHILADELPHIA PA.

NAIL

NAIL

IRON ANCHOR

SCREW

5"x 5" OPENING.
PRESS NEAR TOP
TO OPEN. STAYS
IN POSITION BY
GRAVITY.

FINISHED FLOOR

ELECTRIC CONVENIENCE OUTLET IN BASE BOARD

ration are historical record drawings going beyond the requirements normally expected of "as built" working drawings. As record drawings, they should indicate the original source of each design detail, profile of molding, and architectural feature.

Since they are actually alteration drawings in the normal architectural sense, they should show also all existing conditions which are to remain. Such features must be differentiated from new construction. The drawings should indicate, by note and detail, specifically what is to be done to the existing work and the methods of execution. The drawings should include every existing surface of the building, inside and out, on which any work is to be done. Extensive new framing and construction details may be shown in the same way as in normal practice; new lath and plaster work, architectural trim, or repetitive details may be indicated rather than completely drawn. On the other hand, any new work of a finished nature which comes in contact with original work should be shown completely and the relationship between them carefully delineated.

Details of construction for such features as dormer windows or paneling in restoration work will usually differ from contemporary practice in that large scale details will be necessary to show the exact size and location of individual members. In some instances, manufacturers of millwork will find historically based details difficult to make. They may insist upon submitting shop drawings more closely related to their normal practices. Depending upon the degree of authenticity desired in the restoration, such suggestions may be accepted, rejected, or modified. In many cases it will be found that modern mill practice will be acceptable, provided all visible parts accurately reproduce original work in profile and finish; blocking, thickness of members, methods of securing in place, and so on will usually be found acceptable if done in accordance with present trade practices.

It will save time to prepare sheets of full-size details showing profiles of moldings keyed to other sheets showing architectural details at smaller scale, say ¾ ″ to the foot. These details should be drawn with great care to ensure that profiles are precisely those required. The same molding profile should not be drawn more often than absolutely necessary. When it is desirable to show the same molding profile in several assemblies, the profile, which is to be used by the planing mill in making the knife from which the moldings are to be run, should be clearly indicated on the typical profile drawing as the "knife mold." Each time that molding is shown again, a reference should be made to the "knife mold" in the profile sheet.

Working drawings must be dimensioned, of course, as in normal practice, but it will be found that no building (even our most modern ones) has been built with engineering accuracy. Lines and levels are found to vary and walls and corners are usually out of plumb. It is even more essential than in modern practice, therefore, to note that all dimensions must be verified at the building.

The coverage of architectural details should be complete, even in a building happily found to be substantially in its original condition, because the drawings are historical records. They should be detailed, complete, and accurate enough to provide all of the information necessary to reconstruct the building if, for any reason, it should be destroyed.

The *treatment of existing work* which is to remain should be given very careful consideration; for example, architectural woodwork which is carved or molded and has been painted and repainted throughout a long history will

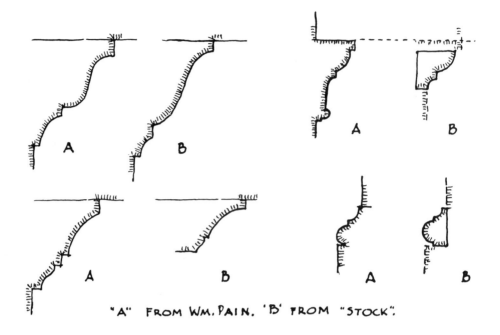

"A" FROM WM. PAIN. 'B' FROM "STOCK".

The proportion and profile of a molding, whether crowning a cupola far from the ground or a delicate mantelpiece in a drawing room, is essential to the character of the building. It is practically impossible to find "stock" moldings which will exactly match the original work on any building (except those which made use of such material when they were built; and even these must be perfect replicas if they are to be accorded the term authentic).

Careful restorationists prepare special drawings showing all molding profiles in fine lines (variation the thickness of pencil lines are not tolerated) which are printed by a dry process to avoid shrinkage of blue printing. The moldings are checked against the original drawings for accuracy before acceptance on the job.

The National Park Service makes important drawings of molding profiles on plastic and manufacturers of moldings must submit their work to a check against the original drawings. Architects in years gone by made the same use of heavy paper called "detail paper."

have lost its original character and achieved another through the softening influence of many layers of paint. The paint can be carefully cleaned off without disturbing or altering original profiles, and damaged parts can be skillfully repaired through the insertion of "dutchmen" or replaced by entire replicas. When painted such woodwork will appear as new, original work will be indistinguishable from reconstructed portions. It is suggested that the paint acquired over the years is worth saving and should be preserved, unless the accumulation of paint has destroyed the character of the work.

New architectural work required to return a room to its original appearance may be fabricated from salvaged old material or of modern "stuff." This new work will, of course, be obviously new unless it is antiqued; antiquing, however, is unnecessary because, if made of the proper material, the new work will blend with the old in practically no time at all.*

From the point of view of the interpretation of the building or its use, it is not important that the casual observer should be able to distinguish between original, restored, or reconstructed work. The student, however, should be able to do so particularly if the new member is conjectural and detailed architectural evidence of the extent of patching and additions should be available.

In the case of painted work, there is no particular advantage to using old material. For work which is to be given a natural finish, it is of tremendous advantage to obtain, if possible, stuff of the same species and approximate age as the material originally used. This is particularly true for flooring and paneling which in former times were of species or sizes not commonly available today. In some sections, for example, floor boards were generally of heart poplar in very wide widths; in other sections they were of rift grain southern yellow pine in widths averaging about six inches. Neither can be obtained today of the same standard. Wainscoting was often fabricated out of single boards, over two feet wide, of poplar and other woods; today these must be made up by glueing narrower boards together and their built up nature is perceptible even after finishing. Chestnut and elm were once used extensively but are no longer obtainable.

It is perhaps self evident, but if to be exposed, the sizes of members whether used for trim or structurally must accurately duplicate original work.

Salvaged Material

It is rare to find whole architectural features such as mantelpieces, doorways, moldings, or paneling, salvaged from another building of the same or similar period, which can be installed without radical alteration in the building being

---

*In more important restorations new members are marked on the back to indicate when and by whom they were installed. It is interesting to recall that this is not just a modern practice, there are many examples of work signed (or initialed) by the craftsman and often such proud mechanics added dates as well. (would that more of them had signed their work)

restored. Changes necessary for re-use usually so alter the character that its architectural value is lost. There may be times, however, when conditions make worthwhile the effort to re-finish a restored building with authentic architectural woodwork fabricated in the period. By so doing, another example of original craftsmanship is preserved for posterity in an appropriate setting. When such material is re-used in a building it is very important to document the original source of the antique material accurately and completely in drawings, photographs, and writing. The documentation should note any changes which were needed to adapt it to its new location.

As has been pointed out above, sponsors of proposed restoration projects who, in anticipation of actual execution, set out to accumulate building parts such as stairs, mantels, doorways, sash, and the like, must at all costs *permanently* mark and identify each piece and member itself as soon as it is acquired and before it is placed in storage; the marks should be keyed to drawings which record and show the material in its original location. Such marking of re-used material may save future restorationists hours of fruitless research.

The architect responsible for the preparation of working drawings for the restoration must constantly bear in mind that he is not a designer in the normal sense of the word. He must be a detective, finding and interpreting clues, and the drawings for the work to be done under his direction must be documented and authenticated in every detail. He must not only indicate what changes he proposes to make in the structure, but why he is making them, and the exact source, precedent, or justification for each feature which is to be added or changed.

Mechanical Equipment

Working drawings for a restoration should also include, in detail, the precise location and method of installation of all the mechanical equipment. None of this work should intrude upon or deface original or restored surfaces. Its location and installation requires the closest collaboration with engineers who are sympathetic with and experienced in restoration projects.* The installation of such equipment will be determined, of course, by the use to which the space is to be put. It is in this area that the design ingenuity of the architect and his engineers will be given full opportunity to express itself.

---

*See also "Climatic Control in Restored Buildings" by Edward B. Boynton, Appendix.

SPECIFICATIONS

A specification for restoration work is like a normal specification except for three things: the scope of the work entrusted to the general contractor; the need for reproduced or antique material; and the unusual requirement for expert workmanship.

The general contractor should be required to provide the labor involved in the architectural examination of the building; the men, tools, and material necessary for the meticulously careful removal of parts; the protection of building exposed by the demolition; and the marking and storage of the parts removed which must be studied by the architect and which may have to be replaced during the course of the restoration. He may also be called upon to protect and maintain the building during the often extended period between acquisition and actual restoration.

When extensive archaeological work is to be done, the general contractor should be responsible for furnishing the labor required for staking out the grid on the site, the rough excavations, the movement of materials, the packaging and storage of artifacts, and related archaeological work. He should be responsible for the protection of excavated areas, the erection of any necessary shoring, the provision of tarpaulins for covering excavations and features during inclement weather, the installation and maintenance of lights when required, the provision and operation of pumps if water is encountered, the equipment and labor to cut down and remove trees unrelated to the former occupancy of the site.*

---

*Trees may often present a real problem. They may enhance the site and yet be much younger than the restoration period, of the wrong species, or in the wrong locations.

The goals to be achieved must be clearly described. This means that the skills and capacities required of the craftsmen engaged should be spelled out. It is not enough to specify that the work shall be in accordance with normal or "good trade practices." The craftsmen must be highly trained in modern trade practices, but must also have an interest and skill in the methods and practices used by the craftsmen of the period of the restoration. Of particular importance are the trades of the brick mason, stone mason, rough carpenter, joiner (or finish carpenter), cabinet maker, painter, and plasterer.

Specifications for brick or masonry mortar are of special importance and must be so written that the resulting work will look like that of the period of the original builder. This may mean that the specification for brick mortar will call for oyster shell lime and a specific grade and color of sand; or, after experimentation, it may be found that a ready-mixed mortar with admixtures of ground oyster shell and a certain sand will produce the desired appearance. The specification must call for the results to be achieved and suggest means to achieve them. (The contractor must frequently be charged with the responsibility of experimenting until acceptable results are achieved.) The bricks in important work may have to be hand made in order to match original work. This may involve the erection of a brick kiln, the provision of special wood for burning therein, and all the incidental processes of opening a pit, digging clay, puddling, molding, and drying the bricks before burning them. In addition to all this the craftsmen needed to operate the plant must be found or trained.

All exposed woodwork or millwork must be fabricated so that its final appearance will be that of the work of the period of the restoration. This may mean that the specifications will mention the type of saw to be used in making boards — circular or band or even, in some cases, cut by hand with a pitsaw, rived or handhewn with broad axes or adzes. Finished trim should not show

---

They may have roots entwined inextricably in valuable foundations or structural remains making the investigation of the archeologist all but impossible.

As with every problem faced in a restoration project, the determination of the fate of trees should be made only after most serious deliberation and evaluation. Their protection or removal should not be a casual decision but should be related to the basic reason for preservation project, how the restored building is to be used, how presented, the anticipated life of the trees and their interference with the accomplishment of the proposed restoration.

the mill marks caused by the knives in the planing mill, but if the work is sanded as required to achieve a good modern finish, it may be too smooth for restoration work. Cautions must be included against ghosted mill marks made by knives out of balance since these defy removal by sanding. Hand planes leave an identifiable mark on finished woodwork, particularly in broad areas like paneling, whether the work is finished natural or painted; hand planing will be necessary for reproduction of such work.

The type of nails and hardware required for any ancient building will certainly require a specification differing from that used in modern practice. The use of proper hardware, both rough and finished, is one of the most important details of a restoration. Hinges, locks, keepers, holdbacks, nails, etc., of various periods and differing localities exhibit characteristics which must be reproduced for authentic restoration. No single detail is more likely to damage an otherwise excellent job than the use of hardware which is wrong for the place or period.*

Painters, in addition to being able to lay on paint without the usual sags, runs, or holidays, must be capable of mixing pigments and matching colors from wet to dry and dry to wet (there is a difference and great skill and patience is required). They must also be skillful in removing paint, coat by coat, to determine a sequence of repaintings or to clean old work entirely and prepare a surface for new paintwork. They must be capable of doing graining, stippling, and other finishes not normally used today.

Stock Materials

Specifications for materials must take into account the desired finished effect of the restored building and only those standard modern products should be specified (by trade name) which are known to produce a result identical to that of the period of the restoration. Such items as sash cords and pulleys, for example, or venetian blinds, or brass hardware, or wall paper, or window glass, wax for floors, copper or lead for flashing or down spouts, stone for trim or steps, marble for mantels, and others can be found today if selected with patience and care. (Do not specify "spot" sash cord for eighteenth century work; such sash cords did not have "spots.") Many specially manu-

*See "Hardware in Restoration" by Donald Streeter. *Building Research* Sept.-Oct. 1964.

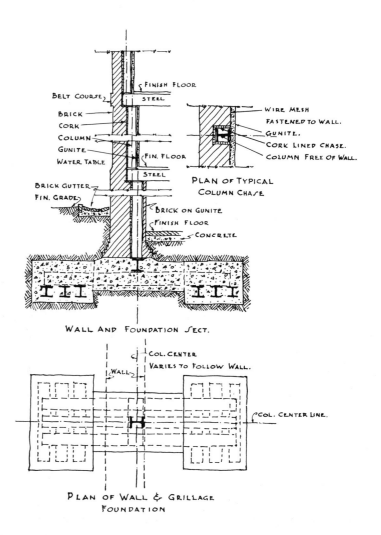

Finish Floor
Belt Course
Steel
Brick
Cork
Column
Gunite
Water Table
Fin. Floor
Steel
Brick Gutter
Fin. Grade
Brick on Gunite
Finish Floor
Concrete

Wire Mesh Fastened to Wall.
Gunite.
Cork Lined Chase.
Column Free of Wall.

PLAN OF TYPICAL COLUMN CHASE

WALL AND FOUNDATION SECT.

Col. Center Varies to Follow Wall.
Wall
Col. Center Line.

PLAN OF WALL & GRILLAGE FOUNDATION

A schematic drawing showing the structural system designed to support the recon-structed Wren Building at the College of William and Mary in Williamsburg, Virginia, stabilizing but not utilizing the walls laid in 1695 which was all that remained of the original construction. The ancient walls were out of line and frighteningly out of plumb but were declared to be in little danger of collapse in spite of having contained three fires. They were repaired and are now tied to a wholly independent steel frame and concrete building erected within them. The new structural frame is carried on a grillage foundation bearing on either side of the old walls which supports a columnar system set in cork-lined chases cut into the walls to absorb vibration or movement.

88

factured reproductions of authenticated items may be essential; the high cost of each work must be faced without compromise

Special Engineering Problems

In some projects there will be need for special underpinning. It may be necessary to install needling under foundation walls to provide footings for an entirely new structural system. Columns may have to be concealed within the walls to support the precious remains rather than to strengthen antique walls that they may support a restored building. Often the loads to be supported by the new use will far exceed those which may be safely carried by original work. In some cases, Gunite or other unusual methods will be found necessary to preserve walls and arrest further deterioration. In others extraordinary precautions (and specifications) may be required to describe methods of investigation to be followed; for example, the transfer or removal of burials, or burial vaults.

Craftsmen, Selection and Training

As has been suggested, the work of restoration must be accomplished by specially trained, experienced craftsmen. They are as much a part of the team which will make an authentic restoration possible as is the historian, archaeologist, or architect and their technical consultants. This is another reason why the contractor should be on the job as early as possible and the men he assigns to the work be those who are interested in history and capable of learning more about early methods of their craft. Manual skills are learned

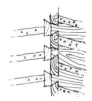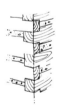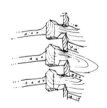

Log cabins may not have been the buildings of the first colonists in the United States but log structures may now be found throughout the country. They stimulate unwarranted appreciation because they look so old. These simple buildings are among the more difficult to date through a study of their intrinsic evidence; moldings are rare, nails are scarce, and in many only the logs themselves remain from the original construction. Some clues may be found in the fabrication of the logs, their jointing, size and method of chinking; study as well the boards and members used in framing the floor and roof.

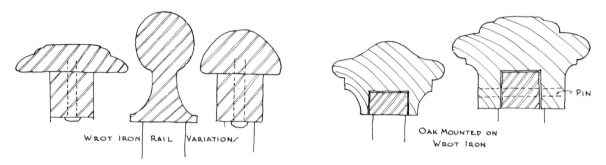

WROT IRON RAIL VARIATIONS

OAK MOUNTED ON
WROT IRON

PIN

HANDRAIL

NEWEL

BALLUSTER

WROT IRON RAIL.

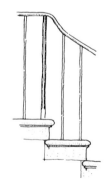

STONE STEPS.

basically by doing and from others already skilled in the trade. Interested student craftsmen should be encouraged to study the handbooks and the work of earlier periods as well as to seek the advice of older master craftsmen. They must be interested in achieving a quality of workmanship identical to that of times gone by. The art of laying out a bond, of selecting brick for headers, closures, or grinding, of laying brickwork with struck, marked or buttered joints was common to brickmasons of the eighteenth and nineteenth centuries but those of the twentieth appear to care very little about art in brick masonry. It must, however, be recaptured because brickwork which does not exhibit all of the character of the period of the restoration fails and will ruin what may otherwise be a good restoration.

In the old days, carpenters erected the frame of a building. Their craft might be compared with the rough carpenter of today, except that the work they did was far from rough. Practically all framing was mortised, tennoned, and pegged and was often decorated in exposed places with moldings beautifully executed by hand.

Joiners of yesteryear were the finish carpenters of today. They executed the finished architectural woodwork, but their skill was that of today's cabinet maker or furniture builder. Practically all buildings which we may be called upon to restore or preserve are, or were, graced by fine woodwork requiring meticulous fabrication of joints and connections far beyond the skill of today's average finish carpenter.

The sponsors of a restoration project who aspire to accuracy should be prepared to assist in the training of craftsmen when restoration-trained workmen are not available. This means that much of the work will be executed by men learning almost lost arts, and that some of their work will have to be torn down and done again, perhaps more than once, before it will be acceptable.

90

This, too, is expensive and adds to the cost of restoration work. It is one of the expenses difficult to justify to many budget-minded laymen, and the latter have important responsibility for a project. Another skill, salesmanship, is then demanded of the architect.

The General Contract

It is desirable to select a contractor, whose interest extends beyond mere monetary profit. He should be engaged on the work from beginning to end, assuming his responsibilities at the time of the investigation of the site.

In addition to the usual general conditions of the owner-contractor contract, there should be special paragraphs added which call attention to the unique value of the building and all of its parts, cautioning the general and all subcontractors and placing responsibility for loss or damage through accident or careless workmanship. The supreme and detailed authority of the archaeologist during his operation, and that of the architect during his, should be clearly spelled out. Practically all work, unless specifically exempted, should be done under the direction (as differentiated from supervision) of the archaeologist or the architect in charge.

The preceeding chapter mentions many of the more unusual items of work which the contractor will be called upon to do, most of which are so nebulous as to defy accurate estimates of cost. The general contractor for the execution of a restoration should therefore be paid on the basis of time and material required to do the work rather than that of a lump sum, estimate, or bid proposal. Contractors who specialize in restoration work may be prepared to give approximate estimates of costs. But, because of the nature of the work and

GEORGE WYETH HOUSE, WILLIAMSBURG, VIRGINIA, C. 1780.

91

the impossibility of determining in advance the actual problems that will be encountered, a lump sum contract is seldom found to be equitable for either the owners or the contractor. It is almost impossible to prepare working drawings or to write a specification that adequately cover proposed restoration work and provide sufficient information for competitive bidding.

Even in those cases where it may seem to be possible to award contracts for parts of the work on the basis of competitive bidding it is wise to have agreements for modifications on the basis of unit costs which may be found necessary or desirable during the prosecution of the work. A plumbing line should be re-routed, or extended because of some unexpected conflict, wiring thought to be acceptable must be torn out and replaced, a foundation turns out to be far too insecure to support the anticipated loading of the restored structure, and a thousand more probable expenses may crop up. (If this sounds like a warning to one who would undertake a restoration, *it is*. A new building may cost more than anticipated, an old one being restored always does, if the sponsors and owners accept their responsibility to the future. "It is better to preserve," but even this operation is fraught with the danger of unanticipated problems the solutions to which always are expensive.)

Although the preliminary work should always be done on a time and material basis, it may be possible in some instances to let out parts of the work (such as plumbing, electrical, or heating) under lump sum contracts and to award other parts (such as carpentry, masonry, or excavation) under cost plus contracts. After the working drawings for the restoration are completed, a lump sum contract may sometimes be safely negotiated for the smaller more straightforward job. However, it would be exceedingly unwise to attempt to do a complex restoration with a contracting organization selected on the basis of competitive bidding; there are too many unknown demands that must be met which will give rise to endless extras and other problems which must adversely affect the final result.

As has been pointed out, the first steps are investigative, searches for clues which will establish the sequence of the construction, the dates of each, the change in character from period to period. No decision made from the superficial examination can be accepted as fact until proven. The beautiful mantel in the front room may seem to be of the same period as that of the doors and trim, but are the doors original, when was the trim applied to the openings? When the exercise of "look behind" is started who can say where it will lead, or how many layers of work, added through the years, will have to be removed to ascertain the condition of the room at the "restoration period?" Nor is it sound to accept negative evidence without searching for confirmation; ghosted marks left on walls and woodwork must be found, if they exist, identified, and reconciled to the final authenticated aspect of the room. There is no rule, no way to know in advance what will be required of the contractor in the period of investigation which would enable him to offer a proposal which is more than a guess.

Similar objections suggest the desirability of a cost plus contract for the execution of the restoration work itself. In spite of the best and most educated efforts of the restoration architect information will come to light during the process of restoring which cannot be anticipated. A new document may be found, the removal of a splintered or rotted board reveal a structural detail formerly overlooked because the remainder of the work all seemed to be of a piece, and further removal and investigation is indicated as essential. The whole design for the area may need revision (as was the form and structural design of the west roof of the Wren Building in Williamsburg when the Bodlien Plate was discovered) or modification of the room in which great events took place may be indicated (this happened in Independence Hall in Philadelphia).

MEDICAL OFFICERS QUARTERS, FT. LEE (FT. DALLES), OREGON. ARCHITECT UNKNOWN, C. 1849. *Individual but of its generation.*

AFTER COMPLETION

Maintenance of a Restored Building

The maintenance of a restored structure is, like that of any other, related to the use to which the building is put. But in addition to usual custodial or housekeeping responsibilities, the restored building must have preserved, in perpetuity, all of its original work.

This simply means that in addition to such normal care as seeing that gutters are free from leaves, that downspouts and leaders carry the water away from the foundations; that roof shingles, slate, or tiles are kept sound, that the mechanical apparatus functions, is properly adjusted and oiled; that painted surfaces are kept protected with periodic refresher coats; that broken parts are replaced; that dry rot and termites are outwitted or discouraged; the maintenance force must consider *each necessary replacement as a minor restoration project.*

It seems self-evident that when it is necessary to replace broken panes of glass, hardware, or other restored items, the replacements should be identical to the parts replaced. Here the source records prove their importance: it is exceedingly difficult, years later, to locate a supplier of a specialized item. And do not forget that the specialized item today may not have been specialized during the "restoration period" but the man or craft who did it then is long gone and a modern manufacturer must be found. The brick needed to match that of Colonial Williamsburg had to be mixed, formed, dried and burned by the same methods used in the eighteenth century, no modern adaptation quite made a perfect match, and men had to be found who had been

94

taught the long discontinued methods. The nearest modern substitutes have been recorded as have been the old methods. The author has never been able to find a modern substitute for the "inferior glass" warped, discolored blistered and misshapen found in old work — except in old work — modern reproductions being usually arty or overdone.

Each restoration project will present its own maintenance problems, when and at what intervals should it be refurbished, what buildings and what parts — research may provide the answer, or common sense if adapted to the conditions under study. It would appear that in no case would the entire complex be given the "complete treatment" at the same time, grass all cut, shrubs trimmed, woodwork painted and so on, particularly if a number of buildings are involved. (Good modern practice would suggest a regular routine for such things as furnaces.)

Practically all old buildings share one major maintenance problem: Floors are subject to the most conspicuous deterioration through the wear of the feet of hundreds of thousands of visitors and the impact of spiked heels. This must be anticipated and given special attention. If the floor is original work and hence has intrinsic value it should be protected from damage with a surface covering or it will be slowly worn away. For reproduced floors frequent treatments with wax or other material may be adequate. But to protect any floors against very heavy traffic, a covering must be supplied. Such coverings should, if possible, be of the sort known to have been used in the house during the restoration period. For example, floor cloth (or painted canvas, not unlike poor quality modern linoleum) was used in many places in the eighteenth century and when worn out is easily replaced. In other areas matting or rugs have been used and reproductions will serve today to protect the old flooring. It is even preferable that rubber matting or other modern material be used in hallways, entrances, or other places where excessive wear will deteriorate and destroy original floor boards.

Related to the maintenance of floors is the control of traffic through buildings and the restriction of access by the public to certain rooms. Devices like rope or chains on stanchions, portable dwarf fences, or fixed enclosures of various sorts have been found efficacious.

Another maintenance problem shared by many buildings in constant use is the desire or actual need to make changes and alterations. Such alterations should, of course, be done under the careful guidance of an architect (preferably the one who did the project) who must ensure that the changes not destroy original or authentic work and that the additions maintain the architectural character which justified preservation in the first place. If the basic reason for the existence of the restored building is the preservation of an architectural monument, no additions or changes to the original fabric should be considered. If, on the other hand, the nature of the monument is such that it might have been added to in its original day, and a real need now exists for that addition, such an addition should be seriously studied.

It is even possible (and this may be heresy) that a necessary addition to an older building might be done in a modern idiom, provided the scale of the new addition is compatible with that of the original work. It could very well be argued that such an addition would be more honest than a present-day adaption of the earlier style, because, if even fairly well done, the vast majority of visitors would be unable to tell the original work from the contemporary addition.

It is to be hoped incidentally, that there may come a happy day when the people will have developed an eye so attuned to architecture that they will rise up in wrath against the real estate promoter who offers "split level colonials" in his subdivisions, and will readily identify such buildings as the otherwise admirable Williamsburg Lodge as a recent, rather than an eighteenth century structure.

Interpretation

The interpretation or presentation of a historic building should seek to bring to life against a contemporary architectural background the person or events associated with the building. The goal is to stimulate the imagination of the visitor to the point at which he can identify personally with the person and place being presented. Rooms should look as though their historic occupants had just stepped out and will return at any moment, may in fact, be just out of sight of the visitor.

Those responsible for presentation of a building and the modern occupants of a restored building, whether public or private, should be armed with the architectural facts related to the building. It is deplorable when, for instance, the office of a bank doing business in a building which appears to be basically or eighteenth century construction is unable to tell an inquiring visitor whether any part or all of the building actually does date from that period. It is even worse when the staff of an outdoor museum is unable to identify for the inquiring visitor authentic or original details.

Architectural interpretation, like that of the social history, should be adjusted to the persons to whom the interpretation is being presented. Relatively broad generalizations will be desirable for school children and the average visitor, whereas rather specific technical details should be pointed out to sophisticated architectural historians.

If the building is of outstanding architectural importance, or contains some unique structural detail or perhaps has been restored to a date much later than the original date of construction, the architectural features should be brought to the attention of the visitor. Concealed features should be made available for viewing by such devices as the hinging of a section of panelling. This, when opened, will expose a section of original exterior brick work which has been covered and protected since the later wing (in the period being presented) was added.

Such devices make it possible to add to the depth and interest of architectural presentation by illustrating dramatically authentic parts in original condition such as: long forgotten fireplace cranes or equipment which have been walled up in a more modern fireplace for years; hand hewn floor or ceiling beams decorated with chamfers or mouldings long covered by flooring or ceiling; ingenious jointing of roof and wall framing members illustrating structural systems long forgotten. Such features will assist in telling the story of the determination of the various dates of the construction because the visitor may be shown the significant evidence in its original context. In some situations it may be possible to leave an archaeologic dig as it was when the investigation was finished; being protected by the building (in a basement for instance) stratification data are well preserved against the elements.

A full architectural presentation should include:

1. The background of the design; for example, that the Plow Tavern was built as a residence by Michael Eichelberger in 1741 and is the only known extant example of the medieval Germanic half-timber dwelling which were once so common in Pennsylvania. The interpreter may then go on to trace the style of this architecture as far back as may be convenient.

2. The basic form of the house should be pointed out; whether it be a one-and-a-half story lean-to, gambril, or whatever; "typical" arrangements of rooms in plan should be noted.

3. Characteristic details such as brickwork, roofing, wall coverings, interior finish, use or absence of shutters, and so on should be singled out and

compared to their use on other similar building.

4. Unique features of the building should be identified; the basic differences between the subject building and those which apparently inspired its designer should be noted; and this building compared to those built by others having similar background and source material.

5. If the building represents construction done over several periods or decades, the parts should be pointed out and attention called to their differences.

6. Original work and new work necessary to the restoration should be identified as well as the degrees of restoration or reconstruction which was found necessary to bring the building to its present form. For example: "the basic log construction of the east wing had so badly deteriorated through the years that it was necessary to remove the east and south walls entirely and replace them. The logs you see in the walls today were salvaged from an old barn on the edge of town: they have been refitted and are installed in the wall in exactly the same manner as the original work."

7. All of the architectural details of the building, inside and out, should be called to the attention of the visitor. Those which are typical of this period should be particularly noted and those which are unique identified. It is this comparison of character-forming architectural details in various periods, buildings, and sections of the country that makes architectural history interesting to the professional and layman alike.

8. The same details used by the architect in dating the building, and in identifying its character and sequence of construction should be pointed out in the interpretation. The manner of forming brickwork around the doors, windows, and belt courses; the use of molded or carved brick; the method of forming joints in log construction; the form and proportion of basement window openings, whether or not they have grillage, and, if so, its form and detail; the profiles of the moldings and their elaboration or lack of it should all be discussed and compared with similar features in the vicinity and with examples of a similar date found in other places in the country.

9. It is interesting to notice the difference as well as the similarities between the work of eighteenth century builders in New England and in the

South. Their several interpretations of the same carpenters handbooks which were used in both sections of the country call attention to such details as the treatment of an external corner in relation to the weatherboarding and siding.

Architectural Record

Interpretation or presentation should, wherever possible, be illustrated by old photographs and contemporary drawings. For all buildings worthy of restoration there should be a completely illustrated and documented architectural record of each part of the entire work telling: a) what was done, b) why it was done, and c) how it was done. This very detailed document will be of tremendous assistance to serious students. The report should not be restricted to the architectural work alone, but should include as well the reports of the archaeologist and the historian.

Whenever possible, copies of such architectural reports should be placed in the Library of Congress Historic American Buildings Survey section. The preservation through restoration of our architectural heritage is important to all Americans because these monuments of the past provide the tangible connection with the present. Their physical existence provides the setting in which we may present and bring to life the great personages and important events which shaped our present day life. Just as a picture is more readily understood than a verbal description the full-scale, three-dimensional, actual building communicates to its visitor more positively and personally the manner of life of an earlier time which has contributed to our own way of life.

Interpretation, or presentation, will bring to life the static exhibit of the restored building itself; it will provide subtle understanding to the casual visitor and stimulate the more sophisticated appreciation and inspiration of the professional.

In a larger sense, the restored building will assure through its mere physical presence a variety and vitality in its surroundings, illustrating the development of architectural taste through the years.

Finally, restoration is fun! The challenge of determining what was, speculating on why, relating the sort of life or activity which took place in the space to be restored to similar functions of our time is one of the more stimulating intellectual puzzles.

APPENDIX

All of the material that follows originally appeared in the September-October 1964 issue of *Building Research* magazine, the official publication of the Building Research Institute. The articles are reprinted here with the kind permission of the Institute and of their respective authors.

Architectural Photogrammetry in Restoration *by Perry E. Borchers,*
Professor of Architecture, School of Architecture and Landscape Architecture,
The Ohio State University. The author is a member of the American Society
of Photogrammetry and the Society of Architectural Historians. He received
his B. Arch. from The Ohio State University, an M. S. in Architecture from
Columbia University, and the degree of Dipl. Arch. from the Royal Art
Academy in Stockholm, Sweden. He is a registered architect in Ohio and,
during 1963-64, he was Science Faculty Fellow of the National Science
Foundation in Sweden.

Photogrammetry, the science of measuring by means of photographs, has
application in all of the engineering sciences. It provides an ideal system for
capturing complex, irregular, and elusive form for detailed examination and
measurement, and its function in architecture, as in other fields, is to obtain
high precision under difficult conditions of measurement.

Process and Equipment Used

Many photogrammetric projects have been devoted to recording material for
the Historic American Buildings Survey of the National Park Service. A description of the equipment and procedures required for these projects will
help to understand the possibilities and limitations of measurement, drawing, and architectural restoration with photogrammetric equipment and data.

The process used is that of stereophotogrammetry. Two photographs of a structure are taken to record two differing, overlapping images. The stereo-pair is used to create a three-dimensional projected, or optical, model within the plotting machine. The model can be scaled and measured in all directions, and, in case of a first order plotting machine, can be drawn in orthographic projection.

Photogrammetric stereocameras take simultaneous photographs with a base between cameras varying from forty centimeters to three meters. Phototheo-dolites, on the other hand, are precise cameras mounted upon surveying in-struments for the taking of successive photographs from widely separated camera stations. The maximum depth of reasonably accurate plotting is 20 times the base distance between the two camera stations, but a greater base/distance ratio increases the accuracy of plotting and measurement. It is desirable to maintain the same scale in both photographic images. This is done by setting up two tripods upon which are mounted alternately the pho-totheodolite and a leveling target. The theodolite serves to turn precise orien-tation angles, to level the camera mounted upon it, and to duplicate any up-ward tilt of the camera axis. It is also used to establish control points within the image at the horizon of the camera.

The camera which is set upon the theodolite is a rigid box with a lens of known focal length and negligible distortion. It is precisely calibrated, and a residual lens distortion curve is prepared for it under conditions of actual use. The focus of the lens is usually fixed; however, the phototheodolite at The Ohio State University is unusual in having a variable focus from 5.5 meters to infinity in increments recorded upon the photographic plate.

Flat glass photographic plates of large format provide good detail in the negative, and avoid film shrinkage and distortion. Within the camera, the photographic plate is drawn tightly against four pressure points at the mo-ment of exposure, and four fiducial marks record the location of the camera axis, rigidly fixed within a box which has no rising, sliding, or tilting lens-board, or swingback.

A few measurements within the picture area, together with the control points recorded upon the camera horizon, provide survey control for orient-ing the plates within the plotting machine, establishing scale, and determining accuracy through calculation of a standard error. A more detailed discussion, entitled, "Choice of Station and Control for Efficient Orientation and Plotting

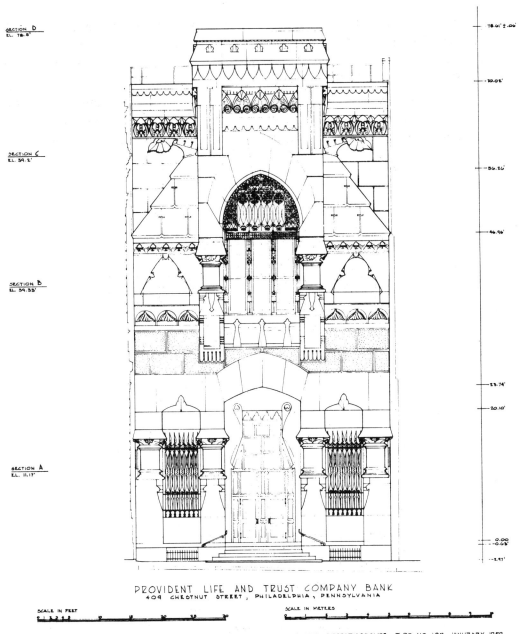

SECTION D
EL. 78.8'

SECTION C
EL. 59.2'

SECTION B
EL. 39.33'

SECTION A
EL. 11.17'

40.55'

78.61' ± .06

70.02'

56.36'

46.96'

23.74'

20.10'

0.00
-0.63'

-2.97'

PROVIDENT LIFE AND TRUST COMPANY BANK
409 CHESTNUT STREET, PHILADELPHIA, PENNSYLVANIA

SCALE IN FEET

SCALE IN METERS

PHOTOGRAPHED BY PERRY E. BORCHERS AND DELLAS H. HARDER WITH WILD PHOTOTHEODOLITE T-30, NO. 182, JANUARY, 1959
PLOTTED ON WILD A-7 AUTOGRAPH AT THE OHIO STATE UNIVERSITY BY PERRY E. BORCHERS, 5 FEBRUARY 1962
DELINEATED BY DELLAS H. HARDER, MARCH 1962. BUILDING DEMOLISHED 1960.

ELEVATION OF PROVIDENT LIFE AND TRUST COMPANY BANK IN PHILADELPHIA, PENNSYLVANIA— *plotted and drawn after demolition of the building.*

in Architectural Photogrammetry," appeared in *Photogrammetric Engineering,* December 1960. And there is a chapter on "Photogrammetry" in the *Manual of the Historic American Buildings Survey,* Part IX, Measured Drawings, prepared by the National Park Service in 1961.

The data on the photographic plates and in the survey control notes form the basic photogrammetric record. This record is sufficient to recreate a structure in a first order plotting machine as an optical model having all the

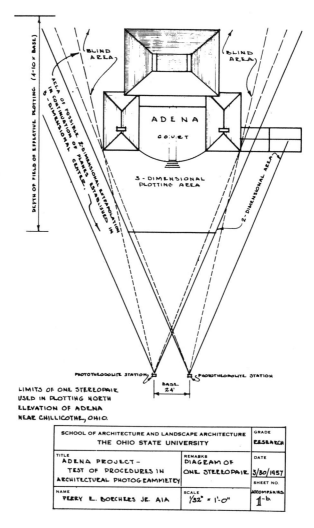

Diagram of the limits of one stereopair used in the plotting of the north elevation of Adena near Chillicothe, Ohio.

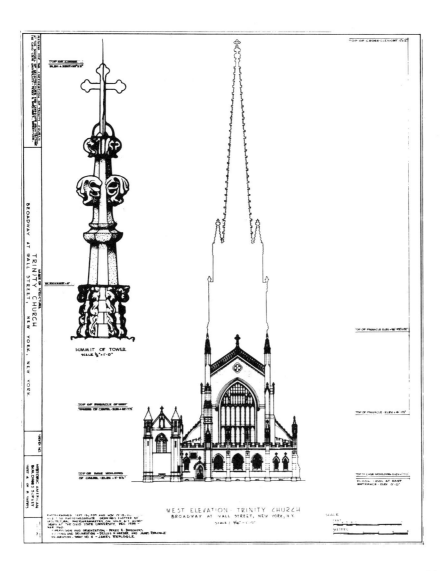

WEST ELEVATION OF TRINITY CHURCH, NEW YORK, N. Y. *with a
detail at summit of spire.*

characteristics and authority of the building itself, for purposes of measurement. The building may disappear, but be drawn in detail years later as has
been the case with the Provident Life and Trust Bank Building in Philadel-

phia. The time spent on the site to photograph and record the survey control for this building was approximately two hours. This is a typical length of time except where special difficulties are encountered in securing full photographic coverage.

Plotting Measurement

Plotting and measuring within the plotting machine consists first of inserting the photographic plates and re-establishing the relative orientation between the two camera positions at the time of photography. The elements of relative orientation include three components of the base between the camera positions, the turn of the orientation angle at both camera stations, the tilt of the camera axis and the swing of the camera around the camera axis at both camera stations.

The relative orientation is then rotated as necessary so that vertical and horizontal coordinate systems in the optical model are in absolute orientation with similar coordinates in object space. The visual model is then enlarged to fit a drawing scale on the plotting table, and the building represented by the optical model is plotted in orthographic projection and measured in the coordinate system of the plotting machine, mechanically making use of the process of reverse perspective.

The three-dimensional optical models created within the plotting machine are the most impressive phase of the photogrammetric process. Separate hand wheels and foot pedals allow the operator to move through the optical model in the direction of the structural elements photographed in the stereopairs. Upon occasion, the major structural trusses of a roof have been clearly located by the slight deflections evident in the roof surface covering them. The plotting table, with its drawings of true othographic dimensions, slopes, and proportions, discloses the intentional or fortuitous optical illusions of architectural design. Scale may be altered in the plotting without reorienting the plates, by merely realigning the reduction gears.

Application to Restoration

The chief value of architectural photogrammetry in the area of restoration is in recording historic architecture prior to change, damage, or demolition. St Paul's Chapel and Trinity Church in New York City were recorded to provide a basis of restoration of these structures in case they should be damaged in a catastrophe. The molded plaster ceiling of Congress Hall in Philadelphia

106

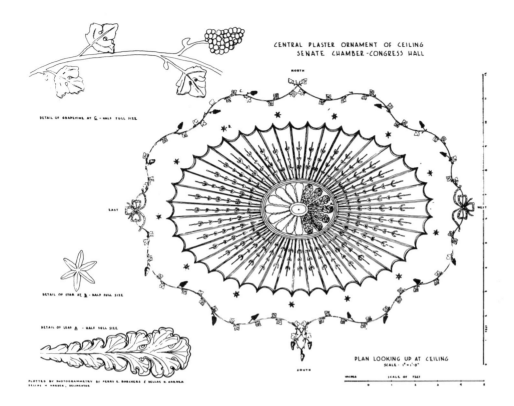

CENTRAL PLASTER ORNAMENT OF CEILING
SENATE CHAMBER-CONGRESS HALL

DETAIL OF GRAPEVINE AT C - HALF FULL SIZE

DETAIL OF STAR AT B - HALF FULL SIZE

DETAIL OF LEAF A - HALF FULL SIZE

PLOTTED BY PHOTOGRAMMETRY BY PERRY E. BORCHERS & BELLAS H. HARDER.
BELLAS H. HARDER, DELINEATOR.

PLAN LOOKING UP AT CEILING
SCALE · 1"·1'-0"

SCALE OF FEET

CENTRAL PLASTER ORNAMENT OF CEILING OF THE SENATE
CHAMBER IN CONGRESS HALL, INDEPENDENCE NATIONAL PARK,
PHILADELPHIA, PENNSYLVANIA—*photographed while in danger of collapse.*

was recorded for the National Park Service when it was in imminent danger
of collapse before restoration. The complicated facades of Glenmont, the
home of Thomas Alva Edison, were recorded and drawn to provide a basis
for large-scale detail drawings prepared for use in repair and strengthening.

Architectural photogrammetry also makes it possible to discover, draw,
and measure surface indications of change in a historic building—for instance, the interruption of brick bonding patterns where an opening has been
bricked in, a lintel replaced, a sill or threshold raised, or where wall notches
for bearing joists have been filled. It has also been possible, as in the old
Court of Claims Building in Washington, D. C., to discover the original form
of eroded and broken mitered edges of brownstone moldings as direct projections of undamaged portions of the molding in sheltered areas.

107

Using Nonphotogrammetric Material

A challenging photogrammetric problem concerns measurement using non-photogrammetric photographic material showing historic architecture before change or damage. Such material may include panoramic paintings hundreds of years old. At least one old view of Stockholm, as determined by photogrammetric studies, was evidently drawn over a perspective projection within the dark enclosure of a camera obscura.

The most promising subjects for photogrammetric measurement are old architectural photographs in the form of glass-plate negatives. These have not been subject to the shrinkage and distortion of negative emulsions on film, or positive prints on paper.

Two other photogrammetric processes may be used with this material. First, there is single-picture measurement, employing a precise projection instrument known as a rectifier to correct for turns and tilts of the camera in relation to plane surfaces to be measured or drawn with details of mural painting, stencilling, or jointing. Second, there is analytical photogrammetry, combining the measurement of two pictures taken from separate camera positions which do not permit stereoscopic viewing with calculation of the major dimension of the structure photographed.

Problems in Analytical Photogrammetry

Analytical photogrammetry with nonphotogrammetric materials requires solution of a series of problems. First is the location of the original camera stations in object space. Second is determination of the turns and tilts of the

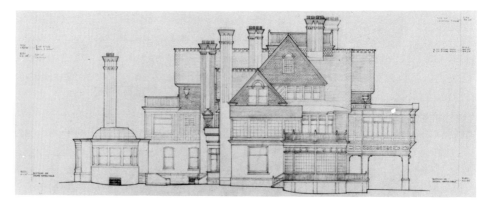

SOUTH ELEVATION OF GLENMOUNT, EDISON LABORATORIES NATIONAL MONUMENT, WEST ORANGE, NEW JERSEY.

image plane within the cameras. Third is determination of the focal lengths of the cameras and the presence of lens distortion variously displaced by the directions of the camera axes and their intersections with the image planes.

These problems can be solved with satisfactory accuracy only when large portions of the building or its surroundings remain to provide photogrammetric control for measurements of the missing portions. An account of the restoration drawing of a dome destroyed by fire is given by E. H. Thompson in "Photogrammetry in the Restoration of Castle Howard" in *The Photogrammetric Record,* October 1962. In general, lines of sight connecting points of different depth in object space provide a fix to determine the location of the original camera stations. Lens distortion is most exactly determined by discovery and calibration of the original lens. The slides and turns and tilts of camera back and lensboard of the larger view cameras used for architectural photography will always complicate the calculation of photogrammetric measurements just as they distort, or improve, the true proportions of a structure in the image plane of the photograph.

In Chicago, The Ohio State University is carrying out a project for the Historic American Buildings Survey which, if suitable glass-plate negatives or other nonphotogrammetric material can be found, will combine photogrammetric and nonphotogrammetric material to make drawings of the complete original form of early skyscrapers now stripped of their cornices and towers and defaced at their lower floors.

With the control furnished by a photogrammetric record and measurement of the main shafts of the buildings, it is expected that drawings of the missing original elements can be made with an accuracy approaching that attained for whole structures with the present rapid procedures of architectural photogrammetry.

Measured Drawings in Restoration *by Charles W. Lessig, A.I.A., Chief Architect, Division of Architecture, National Capitol Office, Design and Construction, National Park Service, U.S. Department of the Interior. The author received his B. Arch degree from the University of Pennsylvania and is a member of the American Institute of Architects.*

A measured drawing is an accurate one, drawn to scale, and based on physical measurements of the subject. Drawings record information impossible to set down in any other way. They are definite and explicit, and include a great deal of data. They show proportions correctly, are measurable, and can be made to de-emphasize existing features, such as later additions, which are not important to the real interest of a structure. Drawings may also be annotated. Floor plans, general sections, and details can present facts which cannot be described in photographs.

Subjects for Drawings

Floor plans are of primary importance. They record the shape, room layout, and location of doors, windows, and stairways, and they indicate structural supports, with dimensions.

General sections are invaluable for recording the construction of a building. They are the only kind of drawings which show the construction of floors and roofs effectively, as well as any unusual methods of support. Sections are particularly important when there are many floor levels. They can delineate stairways in a graphic way. Room elevations can be included in a section.

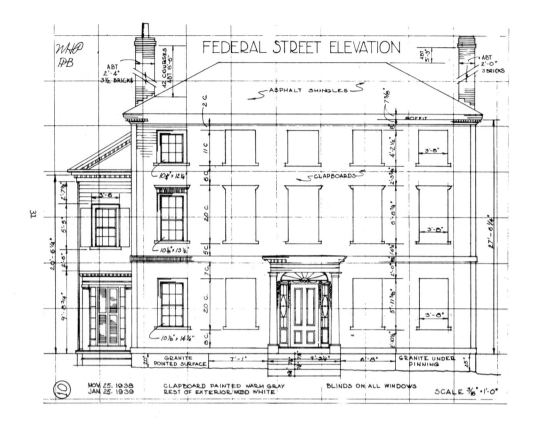

This elevation shows method used for exterior dimensioning and indication of features.

Exterior elevations are drawn of buildings of exceptional importance. In many cases, photographs are helpful in drawing elevations showing the exterior appearance.

Detail drawings are of two kinds, structural and decorative. In order to present the structural type, drawings are needed. Decorative details can often be recorded just as well in photographs, noting some key dimensions. Moldings are an exception, demanding full-size profile drawings. Buildings vary greatly and there are times when drawings, such as reflected ceiling plans, structural isometrics, exploded diagrams and mechanical details, are of value.

Scale for Drawings

Plans are generally drawn at ¼″ scale. Details are drawn at convenient scales but, as a general rule, as large as practicable. There are no fixed rules but

111

interior wall elevations, if simple, are usually drawn to ⅜″ scale. This is a minimum for wall elevations. Doors, doorways, stairways, and interior elevations are drawn to ¾″ scale, while windows and door sections are drawn to a 1½″ scale.

Molding profiles are almost always drawn full-size or, if this is impossible, at one-half full-size. When several details are placed on the same sheet, it is desirable, for the sake of clarity, to draw them at a uniform scale.

Measuring Procedures

Exterior Horizontal Measurements. Measure the exterior perimeter of the building and, from the overall dimensions, lay out the plans of the building on cross section paper in a field notebook. It is recommended that a T-square and triangles be used for small-scale drawings in order to aid in accuracy and speed.

When taking exterior measurements of window and door openings, it is good practice to give the dimensions of the masonry opening for masonry buildings and the center-to-center dimension of sash and doors for frame buildings. More detailed information should be noted concerning sash, lights, trim, sill-to-floor and window head-to-ceiling dimensions at the time the interior dimensions are measured.

In measuring exterior dimensions, determine the overall vertical dimensions, such as the top of the roof ridge to the top of the cornice, top of cornice to the first floor line, and the first floor line to grade. Then determine the distances from the bottom of cornice to the top line of the sash; top of sash to bottom of sash; bottom of sash on the second floor to top of sash on the first floor; bottom of the first-floor sash to the water table which, if present, should be measured and its size recorded; and the bottom of the first-floor sash to the finish grade. Where brick is used, the number of courses should be recorded as a part of each of these measurements.

Note the number of panes and glass sizes of windows, and the number of panes in upper and lower sash, if not equal. In frame structures, note the size of clapboards as to exposure, as clapboards 4″ to the weather, or handsplit shingles, or sawed shingles, 5″ to the weather.

Indicate the floorlines on the elevations and note the dimensions between floors. Indicate roof pitch, the relation of the rise of the roof in one foot of length. Note the flashing and cap flashing if any. Describe the chimney cap and detail. Note features such as roof material, bond and size of brick, loca-

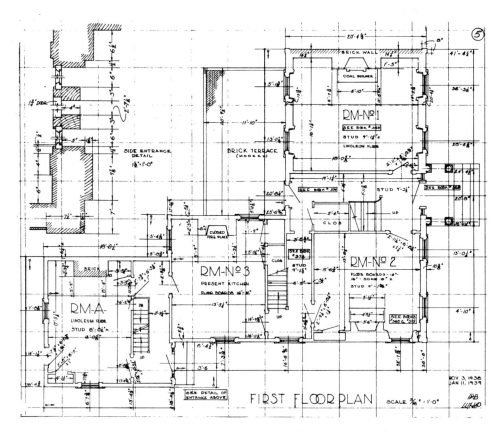

A first floor plan drawn from notes. Cumulative or "running" measurements are taken by holding the end of the tape at a corner or other appropriate datum point and reading successively all desired points along the line without moving the tape. This method avoids an accumulation of small errors.

tion and dimensions of belt courses, and the size of all openings, including control dimensions of the arches and spacing of the columns. Detail exterior features, such as front entrance, cornice and pilaster details, and ironwork.

Interior Measurements. Upon completion of the exterior measurements, the interior partitions and walls should be measured. Where possible, dimensions should extend from the exterior surface of a wall, through openings in partitions to the exterior surface of the corresponding opposite wall.

After the principal overall dimensions are recorded, the thicknesses of all interior walls and partitions, internal openings, fireplaces, stairs, and all other internal architectural features should be measured.

113

Measurements should be carried completely around each room to close at the corner or point of departure and they should then be checked against the overall dimensions taken.

Locate exposed beams in ceilings, projections of chimney breasts, galleries, balconies, cupboards, and apertures in the ceiling. Repeat this process for each floor, checking overall dimensions of each floor against those of the principal floor.

On all floors, including the attic and basement, measure and note framing where exposed, required fabric, later additions, detailed description of fabric, as color of painted finish, type of wallpaper, size of floorboards, and the trim in each room or space.

Detail principal doors by sketching them in elevation with full-size details of panel molding. Detail principal room cornices, window and door architraves, wainscoting base, fireplace mantels, stair halls showing newels, handrails, balusters, stair scrolls, and the like.

Prepare a door schedule noting the location of each door. If the door is

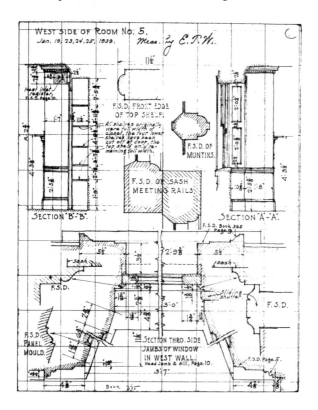

This measured drawing, made from notes as the plan herewith, illustrates the recording of window details, sash, and cabinet work.

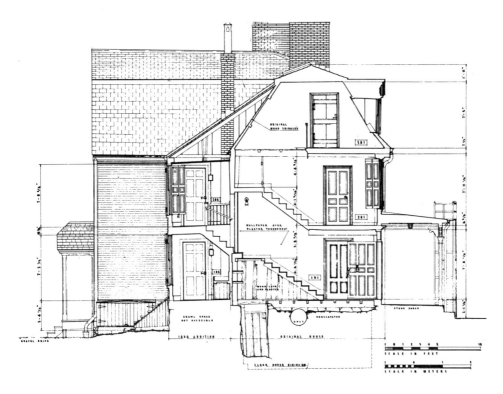

This transverse section illustrates the technique of making a final drawing for permanent records. It is a final Historic American Bulidings Survey (HABS) record drawing.

paneled, note the number of panels and whether they are beveled and sunk or beveled and molded. If board and batten, note whether sunk and raised (both sides) or note the side on which moldings occur, and their size and thickness.

Details, Ornaments, and Profile. Accurate measurements of details are made by determining the overall dimensions and then recording each separate feature. A profile gauge is used to determine the exact contour of molding. Such a gauge consists of a series of thin metal laminations which slide, held together by a long screw whose tension can be adjusted. Along the edge used to make contact with the surface of the molding, the laminations are beveled to a point.

In determining the contour of a molding, the tension screw is loosened slightly and the gauge is pressed against the molding. It is advisable to push each lamination into contact with the molding surface individually, holding the whole gauge motionless until the operation is complete. Then the tension screw is tightened, the gauge removed, and the profile traced on paper.

The result should be checked carefully against the molding itself. This is particularly necessary when profiling small moldings, since the laminations of the gauge are too thick to follow all of the delicate features. As a check, a cardboard template may be made from the traced profile and held against the molding. The template can be corrected until it fits exactly.

When using the gauge on moldings of soft materials, great care should be taken to avoid damage. Some finishes are easily scratched, unless protected by a thin substance like drafting tape or plastic film.

Very accurate molding profiles may be obtained by casting with plaster of Paris. The molding surface must first be coated with wax to prevent adhesion. After the cast has hardened, it is removed and sawed along a plane perpendicular to the molding, thus revealing the true profile. A very fine saw is used, and the teeth are cleaned frequently to assure a sharply defined cut. The method of casting will depend on the location and size of the molding.

Sometimes a molding profile may be obtained directly at an exposed end, or a joint may be open enough to allow insertion of a piece of paper on which the contours may then be drawn. This is preferred to all other methods. In special cases, a building being restored or demolished may offer the opportunity to saw a set of moldings at right angles, and trace their profiles directly.

Whatever method is used to obtain the profile, care must be taken to select a representative section of the molding which is not worn or distorted by many layers of paint. In the latter case, permission should be obtained, if possible, to remove the paint carefully before recording the profiles.

If the actual jointing and assembly of wooden moldings can be seen clearly, in whole or in part, make certain to record the interior details of the joinery to the degree that they can be determined accurately.

Materials and Patterns. In addition to dimensions, materials should be recorded in the field notes. Note the size of brick or stone units in bonds, patterns and courses, and record by detail sketches at a scale to permit them to be clearly illustrated. Note the size of wood siding or log construction. If irregular, give the largest and smallest course dimensions.

Note the color and finish of materials. Note composition, section, and surface appearance of mortar joints, chinking stucco, adobe, plaster, and the like. Note all unusual conditions and materials in sufficient detail to make reproduction of the structure possible, should it be destroyed. Note the extent of the original fabric and where alterations have been made. The exact *present* condition of the structure must be recorded.

Approximate Dimensions. When it is not possible to measure inaccessible parts of a building, approximate dimensions may be established by counting the number of brick or stone courses, clapboards, etc., and then by measuring the heights and lengths of the respective units within reach. This dimension should be noted as approximate.

In the case of a tower or steeple, it may be necessary to measure the height by the use of a surveyor's level and to compute the height by mathematics.

Recommended Practices in Measuring

For general measurements, it is customary to take readings to the nearest ¼", but for portions to be détailed smaller fractions are desirable.

Cumulative or "running" measurements, taken by holding the end of the tape at a corner or other appropriate datum point, and reading successively all desired points along the line without moving the tape, avoid accumulation of small errors. Choose zero points, which will be convenient for later checking and drafting.

Keeping the tape level or vertical and tightly stretched is obviously necessary to secure accurate measurements. Unless lines of the structure are truly level or vertical, it will be necessary to mark chalklines before measuring.

Checking measurements is essential and becomes a habit in time. The person recording measurements should call the figures back to the person reading the tape; other members of the team can listen for discrepancies. Dimensions may be checked by comparing the total of separate units with the overall figure. In fact, it is helpful to do this periodically, because the sooner errors can be discovered the easier it is to trace and correct them. A draftsman's adding machine, with dials for inches and fractions, is a valuable aid when checking dimensions.

A final check of the field notebook for completeness of information, before leaving the site, is good practice and will help to avoid unnecessary time and travel in returning to secure data that may have been overlooked. A later check for completeness will automatically be made as drafting proceeds. Indeed, some problems of a tricky nature do not come to light until a layout is being made at the drafting board, but as a rule one should aim at making the field notes so complete that one visit to the structure will suffice.

A checklist is helpful, particularly for items which should be included in the notes. With respect to dimensions, the final check should verify the com-

117

patibility of measurements made at different floor levels or in different parts of the structure, to assure that they can be correlated.

When the recorder can prepare field notebook sketches in advance of formal team measuring operations, he can place dimension lines, or measurements to be obtained, on the sketches for all desired dimensions. This tends to assure completeness. Similarly, the preparation of blank schedules, to be filled in when measuring, serves as a checklist for the data pertinent to them.

Avoid mental calculations while measuring. Write down the actual measurements taken, and indicate the exact points to which they were taken. On the final drawings, dimensions may be given to other points, which can then be calculated without endangering the accuracy of field readings.

Use of Surveyor's Transit

When a surveyor's transit or transit theodolite is available, it is very useful in measuring structures whose walls are not at right angles, which are not level, or in general where irregularities are present. To take advantage of the transit, the operator must be familiar with its operation. Very accurate results can be obtained.

The transit is essentially a telescope, mounted on a tripod, which can be turned about either a vertical axis or a horizontal axis. In the operations described here the transit is used as a level; therefore, the telescope is kept level and turned about a vertical axis.

Photographic Records in Restoration *by Jack E. Boucher, Senior Photographer, Eastern Office, Design and Construction, National Park Service, U. S. Department of the Interior. The author is a member of the Professional Photographers of America, the Society of Architectural Historians, and the National Trust for Historic Preservation. In 1961, he received the Annual Award of Merit of the American Association for State and Local History for his writing on historic South Jersey. He studied photography at the Eastman Technical Training School and the Winona School of Professional Photography.*

The camera records exactly that to which it is exposed. This is important in the documentation of architectural and historical detail. With the camera there can be no question about whether the architect or artist overlooked something. Everything within the angle of view of the lens is reproduced. Limitations are solely those of the film, equipment, and photographer.

The photographer must present the best picture of a subject by recording details clearly and in correct perspective through corrective photography. Corrective photography obtains a correct representation of three-dimensional objects on one plane, without distortion of vertical or horizontal lines, and with the most pleasing perspective possible under nonstereoscopic limitations.

Advantages of Photography

Photography can irrefutably document the details of a structure. It provides a picture of that which does exist, including variations in texture, tone, and weathering—effects difficult to achieve in drawings. Even intricate forms and ornamental details can be captured in an instant. Photography provides a record not only for immediate reference, but for historical reference in years to come. The employment of photography represents a minute percentage of the restoration cost of a building, but justifies itself by showing that which existed, the work as it is performed, and the completed subject.

Frequently, in the restoration and preservation of a building, entire walls must be demolished and painstakingly reconstructed. An enlargement of a picture of a wall will show each of the stones or bricks in place, with their exact relationship to each other, and it can enable masons to replace a wall swiftly, accurately, and with reasonable effort.

In the restoration of a building, photographs examined at leisure will often reveal details not apparent to the eye, for the photograph condenses the size of a structure from something which the eyes must sweep to something the eyes and brain may grasp at a single glance.

Ghost images of missing walls, staircases and other details frequently show up in photographs. To enhance this possibility, the professional photographer can employ infrared or ultraviolet photography. Details revealed may include trowel and brush marks, or shapes of mantels and moldings. Usually, ghost images are noticed before photographs are taken, but with photographs these details can be studied and related to each other and to the building.

The skilled restorationist knows the value of old woodcuts, steel engravings, and early photographs of buildings. Photographic archives are one of the first sources the architectural historial consults. Old photographs provide invaluable clues about the original structural details of a building.

Historic American Buildings Survey

There is a Historic American Buildings Survey Collection maintained in the Library of Congress. This collection preserves, on photographic film, a record accompanied by the written word of architects and historians. It includes some 30,000 measured drawings and 35,000 photographs of some 9,400 buildings of significance throughout the United States and its possessions. This collection is invaluable to the restorer seeking details of a certain style of architecture or a certain period in the country's development. Indeed, this Survey, inaugurated in the early 1930's by a joint effort of the National Park Service, the American Institute of Architects, and the Library of Congress, has been the sole source of information for some restored buildings.

120

Limitations of the Camera

Photographs in restoration and preservation should always be made with a view camera. A view camera is an instrument with swings, tilts, and other adjustments built into the body of the camera to correct for perspective and distortion. These cameras are available in 4" by 5" or larger sizes. This is the only type of camera suitable for architectural photography. Press cameras are not suitable because they lack adequate adjustments to the body to correct for perspective, and the achievement of great depth of field to bring long lines of a building into focus. The view camera is not a camera the average individual would own, and in any case it is recommended that the photographer employed be professionally qualified.

A skilled and qualified professional photographer generally has the proper equipment and ability to provide a reliable, permanent record.

All optical systems have limitations, be they in cameras or eyeglasses. The wrong selection of lenses can do peculiar things to subject material. The wider the angle encompassed by a lens, the greater the distortion will be. This can happen despite the swings and tilts of the view camera, for short-focus lenses are often dictated by cramped quarters and confined spaces. The correct focal length lens must be chosen.

Choice of Correct Film

The correct film must also be chosen. This is less important than it once was, however, for today the very high-speed continuous tone emulsions used possess extremely fine grain, and the resolving power of films and lenses produces a sharp, crisp image providing great detail. Restorationists, contracting for photographic services, should consider the use of films having a polyester base; however, this does not preclude the use of film emulsions on conventional acetate bases.

One advantage of film possessing a polyester base is that this is an inert material, not subject to the changes that acetate films will experience over the years. Accelerated tests show that polyester base films can be expected to have a life expectancy many times that of the older base films. Traditional acetate films frequently show deterioration, usually yellowing, within twenty years, depending on their storage and original processing conditions and techniques. Some old negatives have yellowed so greatly as to hinder the making of prints and enlargements.

Glass plates may also be used, although they have their drawbacks. They are not subject to change as is acetate but they are extremely fragile and grow more so with age. However, they are very stable, and are used in certain photographic fields because of their dimensional stability.

Lighting techniques necessary to reproduce detail on film depend heavily upon accurate selection of the hour of the day that will place the sun in proper relation to the subject. If the picture is taken indoors, the choice is even more critical, since either available natural light or artificial illumination must be employed and the correct exposure calculated. Such technical factors as bellows extension, reciprocity failure, and exposure index must be considered. If no electricity is available for photoflood illumination, and natural light is not sufficient to place an image on film, how can the job be done? Is the use of either electronic flash or flashbulbs indicated? This is a problem that can best be solved by the professional photographer.

The choice of films in relation to their sensitivity to certain objects must also be considered. Certain films will not reproduce certain colors satisfactorily. In the photography of scenes that include reflective surfaces, techniques must be employed to reveal detail despite reflections. This can be accomplished by the use of polarizing screens and filters, as well as correct choice of camera location.

Selection of Subjects

What is to be photographed in the restoration of a building depends on the degree of restoration to be effected, on the importance of the structure, and occasionally on the availability of funds.

It may be desirable to photograph every square inch of the structure, or it may be desirable to photograph only the elevations or a combination of elevations, the window and door openings, and such details as fine paneling, cornices, mantels, brick bonds, foundations, structural joinings, floorings, and such fastening devices as nails and screws, and hardware as locks and hinges.

It is better to have too much photographic coverage than too little. Not only general views, but specifics, such as closeup views of details in place should be included. It is often desirable to include a scale in a picture to relate sizes. The scale can be a portion of tape or rule; it can be a six-foot long stick, marked with alternate black and white stripes, or small objects can be photographed on graph paper, with the scale noted visibly on paper.

Each view should be identified as concisely as possible. Specific words which are widely understood should be used, and ambiguities should be avoided. Designations referring to compass directions are more specific than words like "front," "back," or "side." Both designations might be used with the common term in parentheses, as "North (*Front*) Elevation."

Use the same photographer to obtain all coverage of a building. He commonly retains the negatives, and maintains them in accurate, numbered files. Reprints and special enlargements can be readily obtained, for years in the future. If the client wishes to retain the negatives, the photographer should be informed of this in advance. An extra charge is usually imposed.

If it is desired that negatives be processed for archival permanence, this too should be arranged in advance. To achieve maximum negative life, it is important that films be processed completely in fresh chemicals, treated in a hypo neutralizing or clearing agent, and immersed in a wetting agent after washing for at least one hour.

Photographs Invaluable

In summary, photography of a structure undergoing restoration and preservation is vital not only for everyday reference but for historical research, just as pictures produced a hundred years ago are vital to contemporary restoration operations. To achieve the ultimate in satisfaction, the photographic documentation should be done by a qualified professional photographer.

Finally, when the photographer is at the site, show him what is to be included in the photograph, and let him select the angle from which the picture should be taken, the lens he must use, and the exposure he must compute. These are his problems, best solved through his training and experience. A comprehensive collection of photographs, documenting a restoration or preservation problem, can prove invaluable to the restorer and to the researcher in the centuries to come.

Climate Control in Restored Buildings *by Edgar B. Boynton, Partner, Wiley & Wilson, Professional Engineers. The author is a member of the American Society of Mechanical Engineers, the National Society of Professional Engineers, and the Virginia School Research Advisory Committee. He has planned the heating and air conditioning facilities for most of the restoration program for Colonial Williamsburg, Inc. Mr. Boynton holds a B. S. in Mechanical Engineering from the Virginia Polytechnic Institute and an M.S. in Mechanical Engineering from the University of Illinois.*

Climate control is the year-round control of temperature, relative humidity, and air cleanliness within a building. Although partial climatic control of restored buildings, including some type of heating facility and a means for controlling humidity, presents some problems, the design of facilities for complete climatic control of restored buildings is a far more complex and interesting subject.

Air Distribution and Concealment

Year-round climatic control for a restored building usually requires the use of an all-air system. This imposes serious problems with regard to the location and concealment of ducts and air supply and return openings.

Because of the problems involved in finding suitable locations for ducts, it is usually necessary to hold the amount of air circulated to a minimum safe limit. Even then, the space and structural problems are formidable as the air ducts must be concealed so as not to alter the authenticity of the building. The location and arrangement of room air supply and return openings in restored buildings is one of the most difficult problems encountered because of the desirability of concealing these openings and their control devices, as well as the need to avoid flickering of candles which may be used for illumination or effect.

In this area, compromises can be made. Many restored buildings are used only for exhibition purposes, and slight variation of temperature in different parts of a room, or even some draftiness, can be tolerated. In some buildings that are to be used for exhibition purposes, visitors are not allowed to enter the rooms, and must view the interiors from roped-off areas. In this case, even cold air can be admitted to the rooms from points in or near the floor. Where restored buildings receive normal use, the air supply and return devices must be designed and located to meet more rigid requirements.

Modern ceiling diffusers can never be used. Sometimes it is necessary to use sidewall grills or grills in window stools. These can be made less conspicuous by omitting of frames and fitting grill cores directly into the structure.

Typical Design Problems

Some of the specific problems encountered in the design of air distribution facilities for restored buildings may serve as typical examples.

Bruton Parish Church. A very difficult and challenging problem was encountered in the design of air distribution facilities in the restoration of Bruton Parish Church at Williamsburg. The instructions were that the system was to be designed for complete climate control.

The structure has a shape approximating that of a cross, with the main entry at one end under a tower. Window stools were about five feet above the floor. Enclosed pews one step above the aisle were to be provided. There were three galleries, one at the rear of the nave and one at each side over transepts. The basement was of limited area and located under the end of the building opposite the tower. As was customary in colonial days, there were graves under the main floor, thirty-three in all.

The design requirements were that air could not be admitted through the ceiling, walls could not be furred for ducts, and the air supply and return openings were to be concealed or made very inconspicuous. Space for a small equipment room was available in the basement.

Because of the graves and the rigid criteria, the problem seemed insurmountable, and it appeared at one time that the structure would have to be restored with no climatic control. The architectural plans for the restoration were complete to the point that actual work was started in the sanctuary before a decision could be made as to how the facilities could be installed. During demolition of the main floor, a brick tunnel, which had formerly been used in connection with a heating system, was discovered extending under the church aisle between the graves. This tunnel solved the problem.

The tunnel was repaired and insulated, and shallow concrete branch ducts were extended under the raised pews to the outside walls at the windows. The walls were chased and the supply ducts extended to inconspicuous grills in the window sills. Return air was removed through small grills under the pews to the space under the raised pew areas and then back to the fan room. The space available for the central equipment was so meager that special arrangements for the fan drive were necessary.

At first, it appeared that it would not be possible to supply heat to the entrance under the tower because there was a grave across the aisle at the entry, blocking all usual means of supplying hot air from the central system. A satisfactory solution was provided by the installation of an air supply fan in the church tower which removed warm air from the ceiling of the sanctuary through concealed openings and discharged it into the entry.

Monticello. Another interesting project was the restoration of Monticello, Thomas Jefferson's home in Charlottesville, Virginia. The mansion has no central heating facilities, but each of the rooms, except one, has a fireplace. It was desired that the building be equipped with complete climatic control.

It was necessary to conceal all ductwork without altering the shape of the rooms in any way, and as far as possible to conceal the air supply and return openings. This was successfully done. Supply ducts were generally installed in chases cut into the thick masonry walls. Return air was removed through the fireplaces and flues in all rooms except one, as the fireplaces were not to be continued in normal use. Flues were closed off just under the roof and connected to a common return duct in the attic space and carried to the basement mechanical equipment room through an old, unused toilet shaft.

The only place where grills are at all evident is in the one room where there is no fireplace. In the principal rooms, where there are wide cornices, long and very shallow grills were located above the cornices and beyond the line of sight. In the bedrooms, each of which is equipped with a built-in niche type bed, the air outlets, consisting of long and very shallow grills, were concealed behind the valances over the niches. The air discharges at a slight upward angle over the valances.

In order to safeguard the mansion from fire, a central boiler plant was located under an outlying building, and forced hot water was distributed to the building through new underground piping.

The Governor's Palace. At the Governor's Palace in Williamsburg, several compromises were necessary because of the building's use. When the building was reconstructed, it was equipped with a forced warm air heating system, and in the front of the building, where there are numerous rooms, the hot air was discharged horizontally through slots in the baseboards under the windows. Since visitors are not usually allowed in these rooms, these hot air ducts and outlets were also used for the admission of cold air, although a deflector was installed to give the air a direction of about 45° upward from the horizontal.

This solution was acceptable for this particular building, but would not be proper for normal usage. The ballroom and larger spaces in the Governor's Palace were equipped with air outlets above the cornices where they were not visible from the floor below.

The Colonial Capitol. At the Colonial Capitol, compromises also had to be made because of the usage of the building. Visitors are conducted through this building in groups, remaining in each room for a very short time. The reconstructed building was equipped with a forced warm air heating system. Most of the hot air outlets were of the floor type, located in the corners of the rooms. For the most part, these were retained in use for both cold and hot air. They have proved satisfactory because visitors do not normally stand in corners. This arrangement, however, would not be acceptable for normal building usage.

Air Distribution and Candles

The design and operation of climatic controls in buildings where candles are used for illumination or effect requires special consideration. The problem does not involve the heat generated by the candles, although the designer must know the heat value of candle wax and the rate of burning per candle per hour. The difficulty is caused by oily, black soot produced when candle flames flicker because of drafts. A candle is probably the simplest and most sensitive draft detector known. Difficulties are encountered in combining candle illumination with even the most carefully designed air distribution, for as the average location of candles is in chandeliers and candelabra, it is nearly impossible to provide proper control without some effect on the flame.

At one time, conditions resulting from the use of ordinary commercial candles became so serious in various buildings of Colonial Williamsburg that the research department of a large oil company was engaged to provide a formula for a candle that would have improved burning characteristics, resulting in less soot emission. The specially manufactured candles now used in Colonial Williamsburg produce about half the soot and drip of the average commercial candle.

For a concert at the Governor's Palace as many as 200 candles are required for as long as two hours. A lot of soot is produced, and is deposited on walls and wall coverings, draperies, and clothes, but the air-handling system bears the greatest load. Even with electrostatic filters of the highest efficiency, a large quantity of soot escapes, with resulting smudging of the supply ducts and air outlet devices. Conditions in the return systems are even worse. It is sometimes difficult to convince management that only that portion of the soot that reaches the return grills can be removed.

Several recommendations can be offered for the design of air distribution and air-handling equipment where candles are to be used in restored buildings. The total quantity of air handled should be held at the lowest safe limit. Air outlets should be located so as not to discharge air directly toward chandeliers and candelabra. All air supply outlets should be equipped with means for adjustment of air stream in volume and direction. All air devices, and ducts where possible, should be designed for easy cleaning. High efficiency basic air filters with easily cleanable prefilters should be installed. Finally, there should be painstaking balancing of air systems, particularly with regard to air diffusion. The final adjustment is made while the candles are burning.

Thermostat Locations

The use of room thermostats adversely affects the decor and detracts from the authenticity of the space. The location of thermostats is always a problem, even in modern buildings, but it is particularly difficult in restored buildings. Where possible, return-duct thermostats should be used. Where zoning is used, and if the air-handling system is operated intermittently, this is often impractical.

In many of the buildings of Colonial Williamsburg, it has been necessary to use room thermostats, but they have been placed in inconspicuous locations and have been painted the same color as the walls. One of the thermostats in the Governor's Palace was located in a closet through which return air passed.

At Monticello, thermostats were located above the line of sight in the fireplaces through which return air passed. They were then accessible for adjustment and were in the path of return air flow. This arrangement has worked well.

Moisture Control

The criteria for moisture control in restored buildings is usually no different than for modern buildings, where the preservation of woodwork, furniture and furnishings is important, except that some curators responsible for furniture in old structures seem to want the humidity held at higher levels.

Some old buildings have solid masonry walls without furring or insulation so that condensation occurs on walls in the winter when there is high interior relative humidity. Usually, however, the problem of condensation is limited to the windows. The control of moisture during the summer or cooling season is a lesser problem. The usual methods employed in modern air conditioning can be applied.

There is a great need, however, for flexibility in the control of moisture addition during the cold weather in order to avoid condensation on glass surfaces and on thin, uninsulated masonry walls. It is usually desirable to provide automatic readjustment of humidistats on the basis of known requirement during the winter.

The reliability of humidifier controls is of great importance, for in case of a failure of the control, considerable damage can result. In important installations, duplicate controls operating in series should be provided.

Refrigeration Condenser Problems

Means for heat disposal in restored buildings presents a difficult problem, because air-cooled condensers, evaporator condensers, or cooling towers must not be visible.

Cooling towers are usually impractical unless they can be located at a distance from the building and effectively concealed. Evaporative condensers or air-cooled condensers located within the building can sometimes be used, but usually the handling of the large quantities of air required by this equipment is objectionable. The use of an external source of cooling water is usually the best. This can be a city water supply where the cost is not excessive, or a well water supply where an economical underground water source is available.

Colonial Williamsburg has recently adopted, for most air conditioning requirements, well water sources which provide provide water at about 67° Fahrenheit. Wells have been drilled in several locations and pneumatic underground water storage tanks have been installed, from which water is distributed to the buildings having refrigerating equipment. This has proved quite successful, and in some areas water has been distributed to buildings at considerable distances from the sources.

The Colonial Capitol refrigerating equipment, which is located in an outlying building, is supplied with well water for condensing purposes.

When year-'round climatic control was added to the Governor's Palace at Williamsburg, a special arrangement for condensing purposes was designed. The cooling of condensing water is by surface evaporation from a small lake adjoining the Palace. Hot water from the refrigerating condenser is piped underground to a point near the water surface at one end of the lake where it is discharged. Cool water is removed from near the bottom of the lake at the opposite end by self-priming pumps located in a small tool house adjoining the lake, from which point it is pumped back to the refrigerating condenser.

At Monticello, an indoor evaporative condenser is used, with air drawn into the mechanical equipment room through a louver in one wall of the basement space under the drawing room and discharged through a louver in the wall on the opposite side of the room. As the normal route of visitors is not close to these openings, this scheme has not been objectionable.

Partial Climatic Control

When heating only, or partial climatic control, is adopted, there are many possibilities.

Radiant heating by means of either hot water coils or electric cables is particularly applicable, because this type of heating can be completely concealed. Fully recessed convectors with baseboard air inlets and window sill outlets, with flush steel fronts or removable wooden panels, usually make an acceptable application. Forced warm air systems permit easy concealment when baseboard or floor air outlets are used.

Application to Modern Buildings

The designers of air systems for restored buildings, as well as for well-designed modern buildings, need more authentic information on the air throw and diffusion characteristics of slots and nozzles. A program of research on the characteristics of intersecting streams of air at various angles discharged from nozzles is needed.

Experience in concealment of air distribution facilities in restored buildings can be useful in meeting the desires of discriminating architects of modern buildings. While climatic control facilities are a very necessary and important part of a modern building, it is highly desirable that they be inconspicuous.

Restoration of Masonry *by Frank A. Smith III, Vice President, Western Waterprooing Company, Inc. The author is a member of the Building Research Institute and the Building Stone Institute. He was formerly with Travelers Insurance Company and the Curtiss Wright Corporation.*

Many things may have happened to the surface of the masonry of a historic building. It may only have collected the dirt and patina of age, or it may have been covered with numerous layers of paints and coatings.

The masonry itself may be in excellent condition if the building's mortar joints have been kept in good repair. On the other hand, excessive leakage may have caused serious water damage to the masonry. If the building has a stucco finish, the stucco may have remained relatively crack-free, or it may have been subjected to movement and volumetric change, and the resultant cracking may have created water leakage and loosely bonded stucco.

If the building to be restored is a brick or stone structure or a combination of both, and if no coatings or surface coverings have been applied to the masonry, and if it is intended to restore the masonry to its original color, several things can be done. If the dirt is not too heavily encrusted and the carbon deposits are not too numerous, a careful steam cleaning of the brick surfaces can be undertaken. This requires the careful use of trisodium phosphate, in a mild solution, thoroughly scrubbed onto the surface of the wall and then removed by steam jets.

The stone may be cleaned by using the low-pressure water and aggregate method, or high pressure water with an aerating nozzle. If the dirt and deposits on brick surfaces are heavier and more stubborn, mild solutions of hydrochloric acid may be used.

A very weak solution of hydrofluoric acid may be used, if care is taken to mask windows and painted areas and to avoid metal components so that etching does not occur. After the use of acid solutions, it is extremely important that they be removed completely by thorough washing of the surfaces with a steam nozzle.

Removal of Paint

Where masonry surfaces are coated with oil-based paints, a paint remover is generally applied and allowed to dry partially. This results in a curling action in the paint, and the surfaces that have been covered with the remover are abraded with a brush. The loosened surface is then removed with a steam nozzle. It may be necessary to repeat this action several times, depending upon the number of layers of paint. Again, it is necessary to steam the wall thoroughly and to rinse it with copious amounts of water to rid the surface of all of the paint remover.

A greater problem exists where casein paints have been used as a wall coating. These cannot be dissolved by any known paint remover. A thorough soaking of the wall over a period of two or three hours, followed by a thorough scrubbing of the wall surfaces with a mild trisodium phosphate solution, will help loosen the casein coating. A high-pressure water hose, using approximately one thousand pounds of water pressure projected through an aerating nozzle, may then be used to remove the softened coating. Very stubborn coatings can be removed with the use of a one per cent sodium hydroxide solution, but this is a rather dangerous method.

If these methods do not obtain results, the only alternative is sand-cleaning. This can be done by utilizing approximately thirty mesh sand under low pressure of about sixty pounds of air. This may slightly abrade the brick or stone surface, but it almost always will remove all traces of the casein coating.

Cleaning Stone Buildings

If the building is constructed entirely of cut stone or rock-face stone, cleaning may be done with a friable aggregate of from thirty to forty mesh that contains no free silica. If this material is impossible to obtain, silica sand of fifty to sixty mesh may be used. Water should be mixed with the sand or aggre-

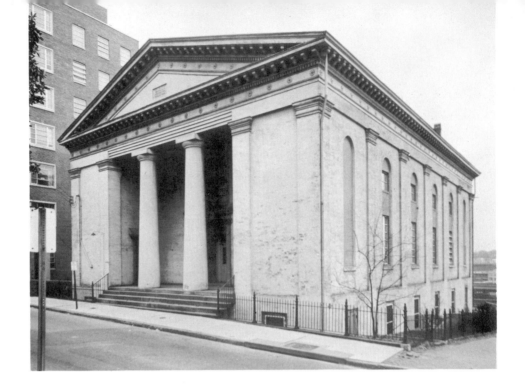

FIRST AFRICAN CHURCH, RICHMOND, VIRGINIA, 1854. *This rather late example of the Greek Revival was restored in 1959 by removing paint coatings from the masonry with a water and aggregate cleaning process. All of the mortar joints were replaced with a uniform mortar color that matched the new masonry inserts. The stucco Doric columns were restored and coated with a cement-base waterproofing compound.*

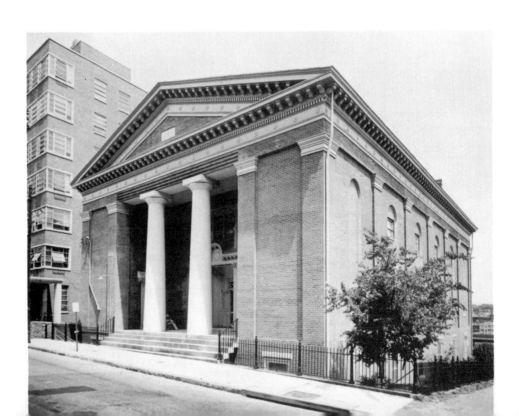

gate, as it is applied under a maximum air pressure of sixty pounds. The cushioning action of the water and the friable material first mentioned as aggregate, or the fine sand mentioned as an alternate, will allow the cleaning of the stone face without marring its finish.

An alternative method is the use of a high pressure water hose after the wall has been soaked for at least three or four hours. The high-pressure water hose is then used at a pressure of one thousand to twelve hundred pounds, the water being projected through an aerating nozzle, which reduces the destructive force of the water. The cleanness obtained by this method is not as great as by water and aggregate cleaning, but it will clean the surface of the stone to a reasonable degree.

Cleaning methods are somewhat different on stucco. Stucco surfaces may be relatively soft, resembling plaster, or can be quite hard, similar to a concrete. Generally, dry or wet sandblasting, with sand of about thirty mesh under pressures of ninety to one hundred pounds of air, will remove most surface coating from stucco. If only dirt and surface encrustation collected over a period of years is to be removed, a light sand cleaning, either dry or wet, with low pressure, may be all that is necessary.

Cleaning a surface may remove much of the loose mortar in a unit masonry wall. This can be beneficial, as the loose mortar must be removed, anyway, if the wall is to be restored. It is necessary to remove all mortar to a depth of ½″ to ¾″. This is needed to restore the face of the wall to an approximation of its original construction.

Replacement of Mortar

Mortars may be compounded to simulate the lime and sand mortars that were used in many of the older buildings. A mortar consisting of one part of Portland cement, two parts of lime and seven to nine parts of sand will closely simulate the sand-lime mortar. This type of mortar gives excellent workability, bond, and plasticity to create waterproof joints.

After the mortar has been removed to proper depth and the joint sides thoroughly cleaned, the mortar joints are dampened and filled. They are then finished with a tool that will form a joint surface matching the original.

A mortar joint, unless otherwise specified, should be a concave joint. This creates the best appearance and gives the greatest bond of mortar to unit. In restoration, the shape of the mortar joint may require study since joints were

135

PROTESTANT EPISCOPAL THEOLOGICAL SEMINARY, ALEXANDRIA, VIRGINIA, C. 1826. *The original brick used in this building had been shipped down from Pennsylvania. New brick to match the old was made in the old kilns near Alexandria and was used in the restoration to replace badly eroded or missing brick. All joints were pointed with a non-shrinking mortar of a color to match the original and all openings were caulked.*

finished in various ways. Some were finished with a flat surface and a "V" coursing down the center of the joint, others with a concave surface. In some instances a flat joint was roughly finished or cut with a trowel.

The color of the mortar must be carefully chosen, for the color of cement may range from pure white to very dark gray-green. Silica or flint sands may be used to help control color, as these sands vary from white to light buff and brown. Certain metallic oxides may be added in small amounts to a dry mix to create almost any color.

Waterproofing Methods

After a unit masonry wall of brick or stone has been cleaned and its mortar joints restored, it is highly desirable to apply a coat of silicone waterproofing material. On brick surfaces one coat of at least a four percent solution of naptha-based silicone material is suggested. On stone or cement stucco a three percent water-soluble silicone water repellent should be applied in one coat thoroughly saturating the surface. Where stone quoins or other stone trim appear as a border, or in the brick field of the wall, care should be taken to keep the solvent type silicone from the stone and the water-soluble silicone from the brick surfaces.

Although waterproofing is obtained through proper pointing and replacement of mortar joints, the purpose of the silicone application is to act as a

FREDERICKSBURG LODGE NO. 4, FREDERICKSBURG, VIRGINIA, 1812. *The restoration work performed on this building in 1962 consisted of water and aggregate cleaning of all exterior surfaces, the replacement of all mortar joints, caulking of windows, and, finally, the application of a silicone solvent to the cleaned masonry surface. Fortunately the lodge had carefully preserved a supply of brick that were made on the site at the time of construction. These were used to replace spalled and deteriorated brick that had to be cut out during the restoration work. It was into this Masonic Lodge, incidentally, that George Washington was initiated on November 4, 1752 before this building had been erected.*

water repellent for the surface of the masonry units. This helps to maintain a new and clean look for a longer period of time by making the surface more self-cleaning.

Replacement of Brick and Stone

There is often a need for replacement of damaged, disintegrated or badly weathered brick, stone, or stucco. These surfaces have been subjected to scores of weather cycles, and in many cases to excessive water penetration, so that frequently it is impossible to obtain stone of an identical color. However, the use of a piece of stone set into the base of the stone that is to be repaired can permit a matching of the contour of the existing block if the complete block is not removed. In this instance it may be necessary to experiment with various pieces of stone to match as closely as possible the color of the cleaned stone.

It may be necessary also to experiment with various cement-based materials that can be mixed into a grout and scrubbed into the face of the stone in which a patch has been placed. This may permit the matching of the stone and patch to the surrounding, cleaned stone areas.

Brick replacement in historic buildings can be even more difficult. These bricks were made of clay and fired in kilns that produced colors and surfaces entirely different from those which may now be obtainable; however, there are a numebr of companies that can match many types of brick. Such a company should be contacted as the first step in the replacement of needed brick.

As a last resort, brick may be obtained from the inside of a wall, particularly if the restoration of the building includes work on the interior. Most often, bricks of the type needed are found in interior wall areas, since walls of masonry buildings are of solid masonry, using the same type of masonry throughout the wall. These bricks from the inside of the wall should match the color of the exterior brick very closely, but their surface will not be weathered and may require abrasion or roughening to match the surface texture of the exterior weathered brick.

Replacement of Stucco

The replacement of stucco entails the sounding of all cleaned stucco areas and the removal of loose, badly crazed or cracked, and otherwise disintegrated surfaces. The masonry to which the old stucco was bonded should be well cleaned of all loose particles and a new, roughened surface for the bonding of the replacement stucco should be created. Stucco may be replaced with gun-applied cement, or with hand-mixed cement to which has been added an acrylic latex binder to obtain good bonding characteristics while minimizing shrinkage of the patch.

After the stucco has been patched, it will present a surface of uneven color. All cleaned and patched surfaces should then be coated with a waterproof coating in the color desired. Cement-base coatings offer the greatest breathing ability and are of the same basic material as the surface to which they are applied, with the same coefficient of expansion and contraction. More delicate shades and a wider variety of colors are obtainable and are more permanent in the acrylic latex emulsion coatings than in the cement-base coatings. Therefore, if color is important it may be wise to use only the acrylic latex emulsions. In any case, a minimum of two applications of any type of coating should be applied to a restored stucco surface.

Sealing of Joints

Flashings and coping stones are very important to the integrity of a wall and to its longevity. If parapet walls exist and are topped by coping stones, the joints of the stones should be carefully prepared. The use of a silicone one-part sealant or a liquid polymer polysulfide synthetic rubber sealant in the joints is advisable. The condition of the flashing where the flat or pitched roof meets the parapets is important. These flashings and counter-flashings must be in perfect condition to prevent water entering at this critical junction.

It is unusual to find calking, as we know it, in openings in the walls of historic buildings. However, since restoration of a historic building may involve incorporation of devices for humidity and temperature control, exclusion of outside air and prevention of loss of warm or cool inside air are extremely important. Windows and other openings should be calked, preferably with polysulfide or silicone synthetic rubber sealants. These are obtainable in many colors and can be perfectly matched to finished paint or trim. They offer as much as fifteen years of flexible life, compared to the normal five-year maximum for regular, oil-base calking materials. Though calking is often included in the painting specifications of a job, it is recommended that it be done as part of the masonry restoration, for it is actually a part of the water-proofing and weatherproofing of the building.

Choosing Method of Restoration

The old appearance of a building may be preserved if this is a part of the restoration plan. However, it is an exacting task for it is quite difficult to match the appearance of natural aging. Under such conditions, no cleaning is involved. The replacement of mortar joints or stucco surfaces is possible, but the blending of the new stucco patches with aged or weathered stucco is very difficult.

The restoration of exterior masonry on any historic building should be thoroughly discussed and planned. Materials or methods to be used should be carefully tried in small areas to test the result of the methods under consideration. The specific methods and materials to be used should not be chosen until tests have shown all results to be completely satisfactory. The methods and materials described in this paper are not the only ones that may be used for the restoration of masonry surfaces. In work or older buildings, it is often necessary to be inventive in order to match the skills and workmanship of the original builders.

GLOSSARY

A selection of words and their meanings selected from those given in "The Illustrated Glossary of Practical Architecture," and "Civil Engineering," written by S. C. Brees, Architect, Civil Engineer, and Surveyor, in London in 1853.

Such books, available to architects and the builders of our early buildings, should be carefully studied because they will often provide the forgotten meaning of terms used in letters, documents, and specifications relating to a building under study. Hand books and glossaries were more than dictionaries and gave detailed if spotty instructions for the conduct of work and the procurement and fabrication of materials.

This glossary is in no wise comprehensive but is included to stimulate interest in such books, of which there were many, by illustrating both the similarities and differences between trade terms and practices about 100 years ago and those we use today. It is regretted that Mr. Brees ran out of words toward the end, Xystos, Yorkshire Stone, and Zophorus are his complete headings under "X", "Y", and "Z".

ACCOUPLEMENT, a timber tie or brace.

ALCOVE, an ornamental seat in a garden, a summer-house, bower, etc.

AMULET, another name for a fillet. Amulets, however are generally situated either over or under large mouldings.

ANCOVE, a sort of ornamental console applied on each side of a door to support the cornice, etc.; they are also sometimes to be found on the keystone of arches, but are usually called *trusses* at the present time (1853).

ANGLE BAR (in joinery), an upright bar, situated at the meeting of two of the faces of a polegonal window, as a bow window. The word *angle* is also annexed in a similar manner to many other parts of a building when occurring in an angular situation; angle bracket, angle rafter, angle rib, angle chimney, etc.

ANGLES (in joinery), the angles of wood work require to be secured together, either by tongues or rebates, as well as nails or screws, thus:-

External Angle The bead in this example is used to conceal the joint.

External Angle This may be nailed from both edges.

External Angle This is considered the most accurate, and is frequently employed for pilasters.

Internal Angle Skirtings, dadoes, backs, and back linings of windows, door-jambs, etc., are put together after this plan.

Whenever the edges of the angles are seen, they are diagonally mitred for a short distance in, thus:

ANGLE STAFF, the strips of wood occuring in the inside of building upon the exterior vertical angles, and employed to protect the plastering. Angle staffs are of two kinds—viz., square staffs and round staffs, called also angle beads, the former being mostly employed when the walls are papered over, or otherwise covered, and the later when the angles are seen.—See *Angle bead*.

ANGLE BEAD, or STAFF BEAD, (See *Angle Staff*); angle beads are made flush with the finished surface of the plastering on each return, and are therefore serviceable in floating the plaster; they are secured to the bond by plugging or wood bricks fixed in the walls by the help of nails. Angle beads are sometimes made to show double each way, forming a *triple bead,* although they are not employed in superior apartments; but the plaster is well gauged, and brought to an arris, a thin copper angle bar being sometimes fitted in to preserve it from accidental fracture.

In the case of an arched recess the wooden angle beads are fixed to the jambs, the bead only being continued round the head in plaster; hence they should always be separated by an impost in good work, whereby the joint is concealed.

ANGLE TIES, or BRACES, the name applied to any framing when situated on the inner side of an angle, for the purpose of tying the work together; thus, there are angle ties to secure wallplates at the several angles of a building, etc. The accompanying cut represents the framing of the external angle of a building.

A. Angle or diagonal ties.

B. Dragon piece.

C. Wall-plates.

APRON, a term applied to the lower part of anything, as to the lower part of a window next the room, also the timber platform at the entrance to a lock against which the gates shut.

APRON PIECE, or PITCHING PIECE, a piece of timber used in construction of wooden staircases for supporting the carriage pieces, or rough strings. The apron piece is placed in a horizontal direction at the ends of the joists forming the landing, and is firmly wedged into the walls at either end.

ASHLARING (in carpentry), the short quartering employed in garrets to receive the lathes extending from the floor to the underside of the rafters, and being about 2 or 3 feet long.

BACK, the side generally occupying the opposite direction to the face, although not always; for instance, the upper surface of a handrail, or other piece of timber, whether situated horizontally or inclined, is called the *back*, and the underside the *breast;* and the same observation applies to the ribs of domes, and to the rafters of a roof. The point of the jambs of a chimney is called the *face*, and the recessed part parallel with it the *back*, the sides of the jambs connecting them together is termed *reveals.*

BAR (of a sash), the thin strips of wood forming the several divisions of a sash, and employed to receive the glass.

BAR (of a shutter or door), a long piece of iron or wood, employed as an inside fastening to a door or shutter, extending across them, and fixed on a movable plane by means of iron bolts passing through them and the frame or otherwise. Iron bar fastenings are sometimes made in two or more pieces, with spring catchlocks.

BARGE BOARD, a board placed at the end of the tiling, or covering of the gable end of a roof. The barge boards of domestic buildings of the middle ages were frequently richly carved and projected beyond the face of the wall, extending downwards in the form of gothic heads with double cusps, etc.

BATTEN, the name given to a board from 2 to 7 inches in breadth, and from five-eights to 2 inches in thickness.

Battens are principally employed for the floors of superior apartments; they are also sometimes laid on the sides of the walls next the rooms to

143

accelerate the works when the walls are not dry, or otherwise. Battens employed in laying floors are classed as follows: 1st or the best, which are selected with the greatest of care, and are wholly free from knots, shakes, sapwood or crossgrained stuff and well seasoned; the 2nd is free from shakes and sapwood, also large knots, but small sound ones are allowed; and the 3rd comprises all that remains after the former have been picked out from the whole lot. The battening laid on walls is about 2 inches by three-quarters of an inch, laid a short distance apart, and the laths are nailed on them, to which the plastering is fixed.

BATTENING, called Soothing in the north of England; the narrow battens fixed to a wall for the purpose of receiving laths and plaster, the former being nailed to them; the operation of fixing these is also called battening. The scantling of the battens employed for such purposes depends upon the distance which they are laid apart; they are generally 2 inches broad, and three quarters of an inch thick, and placed about 11 or 12 inches apart, and in a vertical direction. The Battening is secured to bond timbers, usually built in the wall to receive them; but if the wall should not be furnished with any, wood plugs are then adopted, which are driven firmly into the wall, and cut off flush with the surface; they are also placed about 12 or 14 inches from the centre of one of the centre of another. Iron hold-fasts are employed to maintain the battening against the flues. When any great irregularity in the interior of a room, defect or contrivance, is to be covered by laths and plastering, it is effected by the help of quartering.

BAYS, or DAYS, the name sometimes given to a series of several equal compartments as to the space between the principals of a roof, which is called a *bay of roofing;* the joisting between two binding joists is called a bay of joists, etc.

BAY (in plastering), the distance between the screeds employed for working the floating.

BEAD, a small moulding of a semicircular section, and much used in architectural decoration, both externally and internally. Beads very frequently occur in joinery, being formed by a *plane,* and adopted as a finishing to the edges of boards.

 A bead which projects beyond the face of a framing on which it is situated, is called a *cock bead,* thus: One that does not, but is even with the surface, is called a quirk bead, thus:

144

BEAD AND BUTT, commonly called Bead butt, the name given to framing when a small bead is placed on the edges of the panels in the direction of the grain of the wood, and generally occuring when the surface is even with the framing, as in the backs of doors, shutters, etc.

BEAD AND FLUSH, commonly called Bead flush, a framing with a bead run round the inner edges of the rails and stiles, or those next the panels, and generally employed in the front of doors, etc.

BEAD AND QUIRK, or QUIRK BEAD, a bead situated upon an angle, but run on one edge only, without being returned at the other side, consequently having only one quirk.

BEAD, AND DOUBLE QUIRK, or RETURNED BEAD, a bead which is even with the surface on which it is situated, and returned each way, thereby having a quirk on each side.

BEAD BUTT AND SQUARE, or BEAD BUTT ON FRONT AND SQUARE BACK, a description of framing principally adopted for doors having bead butt panels on one side, and square ones on the other.

BEAK, a fillet nailed under the corona of a cornice, on the outside, to form a drip-off for the rain, and prevent its running down the cornice and frieze.

BEAM, a piece of timber lying in a horizontal position, and supported at each end.

Beams are employed for various purposes; thus, a beam which resists a pulling force, or weight, and fulfils the office of a chain or tie, is called a *tie-beam*. A *straining-beam* is a beam situated between two posts, to keep them asunder, and resist compression; and a *girder* bears an insistent weight, being employed for the purpose of carrying a superstructure, or any superincumbent weight, as a wall, or a floor, etc. A beam laid on an external wall is distinguished as a *bressummer*. The term girder, however, has almost supplanted all others for beams of this description, whether of iron or wood; it refers, however, more particularly to those lying across the building; and a beam tenoned into the middle of a girder, for the purpose of supporting the joists of a floor, somewhat similar to a binding joist, was formerly called a *summer,* and much employed.

BELECTION, or BALECTION MOULDINGS, the projecting mouldings run around any framing, and which are generally placed next the panels and laid on the framing. Belection mouldings are principally employed at the present time for external doors and costly wainscoting (1853).

BINDERS, or BINDING JOISTS, the joists employed to carry common joists where the distance across the apartment is more than usual, and which have the effect of shortening their bearings. Girders are sometimes used to support binding joists in very large rooms — (See *Girder*). The ceiling, in this case, is formed upon small joists, termed ceiling joists, which are usually secured to the lower edges of the binding joists, being either notched and nailed thereto, or framed to them flush with the under side of the said joists, by means of pulley and chace mortices: it is also necessary to fir the under side of the girders as may be required, to correspond with the under side of the ceiling joists. Double framed floors have also the advantage of preventing the sound passing from one story to another, and preserving the ceiling from cracks and irregularities.

Binding joists should not be more than six feet apart, and of the following scantlings:

Length of Bearing	Depth	Width
Feet	Inches	Inches
6	6	4
8	7	4½
10	8	5
12	9	5½
14	10	6

[the table continues]

The girders employed in carrying the binders or binding joists should each be placed about 10 feet apart, and of the following scantlings:

Length of Bearing	Depth	Width
Feet	Inches	Inches
10	9	7
12	10	8
14	11	9
16	12	10
18	12	11
20	13	11
22	14	12

[the table continues]

BIRD'S MOUTH (also called a Sally), the name applied to a notch cut at the end of a piece of wood, or otherwise, and forming an internal angle to a rafter whereby it is enabled to rest upon the pole plate, or other timber. It is also applied to interior angles in brickwork, etc.

BLIND AREA, an area built around a basement wall to keep it dry.

BOARDS, the name given to flat pieces of timber generally, but applying more particularly to pieces of stuff exceeding 4½ inches in breadth, and under 2½ inches in thickness. Fir boards that are 9 inches in breadth are called *deals,* and boards of greater breadth, *planks,* as pine timber. When a series of boards are joined or laid together side by side, the edges are either planed, technically called *edges shot,* or the edges are shot and then ploughed and tongued; and when the side surfaces are planed they are described as *wrought;* thus, flooring boards are generally prepared by being wrought on one side, the other being left rough and the edges shot. Where two or more pieces of board are required to be joined together edgeways, it is accomplished by pins or nails, or by ploughing and tonguing the edges, if the thickness admit of it; otherwise the edges are glued; white lead, mixed with linseed oil, being used for external work. Boards which are much thicker on one edge than the other are called *feather-edged boards.*

BOARD AND BRACE FRAMING, a mode of framing, consisting of battens placed vertically, and grooved in the edges, into which thin deal boards are inserted.

BOASTING (in carving), a term applied to the carving of any ornament, etc., at that stage when they are just roughed out and brought to their proper contour, previous to the commencement of the raffles and other details. [*one wonders why 'raffles' is not anywhere defined*]

BOND, or BOND TIMBERS, the timbers built in walls in a horizontal position, for the purpose of strengthening the building, and tying it together during the course of construction. They are also generally employed for securing the battening and bracketing to, if there be any. The whole of the timbers in a building acting as ties are also known as bond, as the plates, etc.

Bond timbers are of two kinds — 1st, *Principal bond,* which is used to connect a building together, and is very servicable in bad soil, by preventing the occurence of cracks and settlements in the event of the foundation giving way. . . . The second description is called *common bond,* and is used for the purpose of fixing the interior finishings; it is therefore disposed entirely to suit the mode in which the apartments are intended to be finished—viz., at the height of the skirting, etc. . . .

BOXINGS (of window shutters), the cases on each side of a window, in which each half of the shutters is folded and deposited in the day time, when the

147

window is not inclosed by them. The boxing consists of a front architrave, which is frequently laid on a ground flush with the plastering, and a back lining, which is laid against the window jambs; one end is tongued into the inside lining of the sash frame, and the other into the ground next to the architrave. . . .

BRACKETING, an arrangement of wooden brackets employed as a skeleton support to mouldings and other ornamental details, when formed in plastering. It is by means of bracketing that the fanciful work so much employed in the upper parts of apartments at the present time, is accomplished; as arches, domes, sunk panels, coves, pendentine work, etc. The brackets are usually placed about twelve inches apart, with angular ones at all corners, and cut to suit the section of the moulding, or other body to be formed on them, and from three-quarters of an inch to seven-eighths or one inch from the finished face of the plastering; the lathing is nailed to the brackets which complete the skeleton of the mouldings, or whatever it may be, and upon this the plastering is laid. It will therefore be perceived that bracketing is unnecessary for small mouldings, but it effects a considerable saving in plaster in large ones.

BRICK-NOG PARTITION, or NOGGING, a description of walling consisting of brickwork and timber. It is usually made of the width or thickness of a brick, and is framed similar to a wood partition, the quarters or studs being two or three feet apart, with brickwork filled in between them; horizontal pieces, called *nogging pieces,* are also laid in regular tiers between every two courses of bricks. Although brick nogging does not add to the strength of a partition, it is some little security against fire.

BRING UP, a term used by workmen in various ways: thus, the foreman gives instructions to the bricklayers (in reference to a wall), to *bring* it *up* to the height of the floor joists, etc. Painters also speak of a room requiring another coat of paint to *bring up* the colour etc.

BUTTING JOINT (in carpentry), a joint formed by two pieces of timber when the fibres of one are perpendicular, or inclined to those of the other—thus the foot of a principal rafter buts on the tiebeam. If the width of the tiebeam admits of it, the whole thickness of the rafter should be let in with a circular abutment, otherwise the annexed plan may be followed.

BUTTON, a small piece of wood or metal fastened to a door or other closure by a screw in the centre, and serving the purpose of a fastening to the door, upon being turned a quarter of a revolution.

BUTTON (of a lock or a bolt), a round metal head, serving as a handle for moving the bolt of a lock or bolt.

CABLE, a moulding resembling a rope or ornamental stuff, and laid in the lower portion of the flutes of columns, etc.

CAMBER, a word referring, according to Mr. Peter Nicholson, to "an arch on the top of an aperture," hence the term *camber windows, camber beams,* etc., being such as are slightly arched upwards. The tie beams of a roof are always cambered a trifle, as an allowance for the sinking which occurs after they are fixed. The beams employed in supporting a lead flat are also sometimes cut on the upper edge, and formed with a declivity each way, for the purpose of carrying off the rain water, and are termed *camber beams.*

CAMP CEILING, a description of a ceiling generally adopted for rooms formed in the roof of a building, in which a portion of the ceiling is inclined like the top of a tent, excepting that they are flat instead of curved, as they follow the line of the rafters, the middle area of the ceiling remaining level.

CANT, or CANTED, a term applied by workmen to a wall that forms an angle with the face of another wall. A moulding is also described as *canted,* when formed without any quirks or circular work, consisting merely of an oblique face. The flutes of columns are sometimes formed in cants, when they are called *canted columns.*

CARCASE (of a building), the naked shell of a house, without either floors, joiner's work, or plastering.

CARPENTRY, the art of constructing and fixing the principal timbers of an edifice, as the sleepers, planking, and piling, employed in the foundations of structures; also the joisting, roofing, naked flooring, centering, battening, etc., and all the rough wood work of buildings generally. The carpenters work is the chief tie and connexion of a building, it forms the ligaments which bind the walls together.

CARRIAGE (of wooden stairs), the pieces supporting the steps. A flight of stairs by the side of a wall is furnished with two carriages, or *rough strings,* inclined to suit the pitch. The carriage of two flights, with a half space situated between, consists of a beam parallel to the risers of the steps, the several joists which carry the floor-boards being framed into it. This is called an *apron-piece,* and the part which receives the upper ends of the rough strings a *pitching-piece*: the joists are either tenoned into or otherwise bridge over it. The upper ends of the string-pieces rest against another apron-piece at the landing.

CASE (of stairs), the name applied to the wall enclosing the staircase, from which it would appear that those carried up without any, and isolated, or with a wall on one side or two sides only, as may sometimes be observed, should be called *stairs,* and not staircase.

CASED, a term signifying the covering or enclosing of anything, thus walls are sometimes cased with stone or brick of superior quality to that forming the interior; the weights of sash frames are also generally enclosed for the purpose of concealment, and are hence called *cased sash frames.*

CISTERN, a receptacle for containing water, and usually made of boarding, lined with sheet lead, and soldered angles. Slate cisterns are much used at the present time (1853).

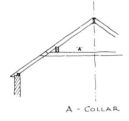

COLLAR BEAM, a timber sometimes occuring in the construction of roofs, being employed in a similar manner to a tie beam; viz., to tie the two sides together; it does not, however, extend as far as the walls, but is secured to the lower part of the rafters; like the tie beam, it is always in a state of tension.

A - COLLAR

The purlins are usually rested upon the collars in common roofing.

COMPOSITION ORNAMENTS, a certain kind of plaster ornament, consisting of whiting, glue, and linseed oil, etc., mixed in certain proportions, and formed by being compressed in proper moulds. Composition is much employed in connexion with wood work; as for bosses, pateras, capitals, etc. Paper maché however, has superseded it in some cases, and gutta percha and stamped leather in others.

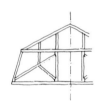

CONCRETE, an artificial cement composed of lime and gravel, or sand, and in high repute at the present time for the foundations of structures. It was first used in the year 1815, by Mr. Ralph Walker, E. E. at the West India Docks, and subsequently at the Custom House of London, after piles had failed. . . .

COUNTER LATH, a lath placed by eye equidistant between two gauged ones, and which usually occurs in roofing; the laths are consequently alternately gauged and countered.

CROWN GLASS, the finest kind of window glass, plate glass excepted. Newcastle crown glass is the most esteemed.

CUPOLA, a lantern or small apartment, either circular or polygonal,and situated on a dome.

CURB ROOF, also called MANSARD ROOF, a roof formed with canted slopes; curb roofs are adopted for the purpose of obtaining height and space within, which is appropriated for dormitories, and usually consist of two planes on each side of the ridge, instead of being sloped down in one. The uppermost rafters are *curb rafters,* and the plate on which they rest the *curb plate.*

CURTAIL STEP, a name given to the bottom step of a staircase when finished with a scroll end similar to the handrail.

CUT BRACKETS, a bracket formed out of a portion of a board, and curved on the edge. The annexed cut shows how two brackets may be formed with one cut, so that no stuff is wasted.

DADO, or DIE, a plain flat face situated between a base and a capping, as the *die of a pedestal.*

That part of the wall of a room situated between the base and surbase is also called a *dado,* and was much adopted formerly, but as a surbase is seldom employed now, the dado consequently does not occur; when it does it is plain, and composed of plaster, although panels are usually met with in old wooden dadoes.

DEAL, a fir board about 3 inches in thickness, and seldom exceeding 9 inches in breadth.

Deals are imported from abroad, where they are cut into the proper thicknesses by machinery; those from Norway are the best for framing; Christiana are the most used for floors. The stuff is afterwards cut down in this country into boards of various thicknesses, to suit the purposes required, and is called according to the number of its subdivisions, as *three-cut stuff,* etc.; *whole deal* is 1¼ inches thick, and *slit deal* half that thickness. . . .

DORMER, or DORMANT, a window made in the sloping sides of a roof, the frame being placed in a vertical position, and placed upon the rafters. The top of a dormer is mostly covered with a piece of lead, the sides being composed on lath; they are also sometimes covered with slates.

DOUBLE MARGIN DOOR, a door formed in imitation of a folding door, the middle style being formed double, and which are separated by a bead, which is called a staff bead.

DOUBLE HUNG WINDOW, a window consisting of two sashes, each being hung with lines, weights, and pullies.

DRAW-BORE, a mode of pinning a mortice and tenon, the hole being made nearer to the shoulder in the latter, which has the effect of bringing it closer home.

DRESSING (in joinery), a term applied to any moulding or finishing.

DUBBIN, or DUBBING OUT, the filling in coarse stuff to any irregularities or decayed parts in the face of a wall previous to finishing it, either in cement or otherwise.

DWARF WALL, a wall of less height than the story of the building to which it belongs. The walls employed in supporting the basement floors of houses are also called *dwarf walls,* and are usually rested upon oak plates and sleepers, as fir timber is more likely to be affected by the damp; the walls are made about 2 feet high and 14 inches thick, with two courses of footings, and the plates are bedded upon them, and they are placed about 6 or 8 feet apart. Oversailing courses are sometimes constructed in the walls to carry the plates lying next them, instead of bearing walls. The walls supporting iron railings are designated *dwarf walls*

EAVES BOARD, LATH, or CATCH, called *doubling* in Scotland, an arris fillet, or thick feather-edged board, fixed round the eaves of a building, to raise the bottom of the first course of slates, and thus give the requisite tilt to the courses over it.

EDGES SHOT, the term applied when the longitudinal edges of any boards are planed and fitted together as floor boards generally are.

ELBOWS, the two small pieces of framing which occur on each side of a window immediately below the shutters, when the window jambs are carried down to the floor, forming a slight recess in the room. They are of similar height to the window back, and tongued or rebated into it. The sides or flanks or any framing or panelled work are also known by the name of *elbows.*

ELM, an English wood formerly in general use for water-pipes. It may be employed for piles provided they are constantly under water, but will not stand alternate dryness and moisture. It bears the drift of bolts and nails better than any other timber. A cubic foot weighs 36 lbs.

ENTRESOLE, a story or portion of a story, of small height compared with that of the principal floors, and occuring in such situations where the rooms are not required to be very high.

ESTRADE, a sort of platform occurring in a room, but very slightly raised; it is usually set apart for distinguished visitors.

EYE (of a dome), the circular aperture in the top to admit light and air.

FACING, the external covering of front walls, which is generally of a better material than the interior; great care should be taken to bind the facing and backing of a wall together.

FEATHER-EDGED, a term applied to any feature or appendage thinner on one edge than on the other; thus deal boards are sometimes *feather-edged,* two boards being sawed out of a piece of stuff of very little larger scantling than the thicker edge.

152

Feather-edged boards are formed for covering roofs, facing wooden buildings, boards, palings, etc., and are also known by the name of *weather boarding;* they are generally left rough, and painted or tarred over.

FINE STUFF, the mortar employed as the finishing coat in plastering the ceilings and inside walls of common houses. It consists of lime slacked with a small quantity of water, and a little fine sand is accordingly added, and sifted through a fine sieve. It is kept in a tub, or oblong box, in a semifluid state, until the water has nearly evaporated; a small portion of hair is sometimes mixed with it. A thin coat of the fine stuff is laid over the first coat of plastering, and which operation is called *setting.*

FINISHING COAT, the third and last coat in plastering; when the last coat if formed for paint, it is executed very carefully, and called *stucco;* if for paper it is composed of fine stuff, and called *setting.*

FIR-FRAMED, this term refers to such timber framing as is left rough or unwrought, as rafters, joists, quarters, etc.

FIRST COAT, the primary coat in plastering, consisting of plaster, or coarse stuff. The first coat of a two-coat work, is called *laying* when executed on lath, and *rendering* when on brick; but in three-coat work, *pricking up* is substituted for the former, and *roughing in* for the latter.

FISHED BEAM, a beam bellying on the underside.

FLATTING, (in painting), a description of finishing adopted in superior apartments of houses only, presenting a beautiful dead white, gray, or fawn colour, perfectly flat and even, and without gloss which accompanies ordinary painting; it also preserves the colour for many years.

FLEMISH BRICKS, a description of brick employed for paving offices and yards, and very similar to Dutch clinkers.

FLIGHT, a series of parallel steps, carried in the same direction without either landings, spaces, or winders between them. The whole of the stairs from one floor to another are sometimes erroneously called by this name, although they are but seldom comprised in less than two flights, the lower one should be designated the *leading flight,* and the upper one the *returning flight.*

FLOATING, a term employed in plastering, and referring to the levelling of the surface for both walls and ceilings. The floating always forms the second coat, although trowelled stucco is also floated, etc.; hence the term floating implies the pricking up as well, or roughing in, as the case may be. . . .

FOX TAIL WEDGING, a certain mode of securing mortice and tenon work, consisting of a compound wedge. The mortice is formed of a dovetailed shape,

153

and the tenon has wedges let into the end, and as it is driven these wedges meet the end of the mortice, and thus penetrate into the ends of the tenon, splitting it, and causing it to take the dovetailed shape like that of the mortice.

FRAMING, (in joinery), such woodwork as is framed.

The framing employed in joinery is of various descriptions, as square, bead butt, bead flush, bead and quirk, bead and double quirk, etc., each of which will be found under their respective heads, and are represented in the following cuts.

A - PLAN OF MORTISE
B - WEDGE AFTER DRIVING
C - WEDGES BEFORE DRIVING

A.   B.   C.

The panels are sometimes raised, which gives increased strength to the framing, and renders them better adapted for external doors.

FRANKING, the notching out a certain portion of a sash-bar for the passage of the transverse bar, and which thereby become mitred together. No more should be cut away than absolutely necessary, so that the strength of the bar be not unnecessarily weakened.

FREE or FROWEY STUFF, a term applied to stuff that is soft and easily wrought, and which takes the plane without tearing, as deal.

FRENCH SASHES, or CASEMENTS, a window with the sashes hung like folding doors. The sashes of Gothic windows should always be made upon this system, to give proper effect to the style. The upper part, or head, may be fixed, if desirable, the lower part only being made to open.

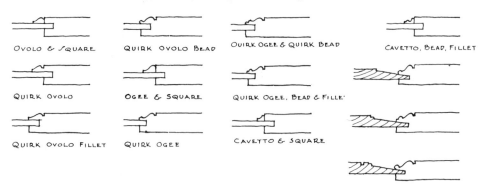

OVOLO & SQUARE   QUIRK OVOLO BEAD   QUIRK OGEE & QUIRK BEAD   CAVETTO, BEAD, FILLET

QUIRK OVOLO   OGEE & SQUARE   QUIRK OGEE, BEAD & FILLE'

QUIRK OVOLO FILLET   QUIRK OGEE   CAVETTO & SQUARE

FRETWORK (in glazing), a term given to the filling-in of a window, when composed of a number of separate pieces of stained and ground glass, fitted

154

together in fine lead, and of different patterns, family arms, armorial bearings, and other devices being worked in it.

FRONTON, or FRONTISPIECE, a name given to the decorated entrance to a building, consisting of a cornice supported by consoles and surmounted with a pediment or some other embellishment. It also sometimes bears reference to the entire face or front of a building.

FURNITURE, the several articles in ironmongery connected with the finishing of apartments; as the brass knobs connected with the locks of doors, windows, and shutters.

FURRING, the operation of nailing thin pieces of lath or wood upon the edges of parallel timbers, to bring them to a level surface, such small pieces of stuff being called *furs*. The several joists of a floor frequently require *furring* before the floor-boards can be laid down, and old floors always undergo it when new boarding is required, as they are generally sagged. Rafters and ceiling joists also sometimes require it, when they are said to be *furred up*.

GABLE, or GABLE END, the name given to the triangular piece of walling at the end of a roof extending from the eaves to the ridge, and filling the space between the raising-plate and the rafters, and consequently cannot occur unless the ridge and rafters are continued to the face of the end wall.

GATES, the open framed doors situated at the entrances of parks and gardens, which usually consist of bars of iron or wood secured together. Gates are hung upon posts termed *gate-posts,* which they shut against.

The hanging-post of a gate should be made stouter than the projecting end, and it ought to be formed as light as possible, as the weight tends to shatter and destroy the gate in shutting.

GAUGE, or GAUGE STUFF, a stiff and compact plaster, and mostly employed for cornices, mouldings, and all other members that are run with a mould, also for the ceilings of superior apartments, and sometimes for setting walls. It consists of two-fifths of fine stuff, and one fifth of plaster of Paris, mixed with a very small quantity of water. The plaster of Paris has the effect of setting or fixing the work quickly, hence workmen gauge the whole of their plaster when time is an object. Gauge is also sometimes composed of coarse stuff and plaster, and of putty and plaster.

GATHERED OVER, the term applied to a flue when it is carried over a short distance to the chimney stack.

GAUGE, or GAGE (of tiling and slating), a term referring to the distance which the several courses are apart; that portion of a tile which appears below the lap, or is uncovered by the course above, is called the *gauge of the course.*

GEOMETRICAL STAIRCASE, a staircase formed of stone, in which the steps are secured in the walls at one end only, the other forming a continued string. Stone steps should not be tailed into the walls less than 9 inches, and this part should always be laid square and solid, although the underside of the steps may be feather-edged.

GIN, or GYN, a machine for raising weights, as machinery, and the stones used in building, also large guns on to their carriages.

It consists of three round legs of 12 or 13 feet long, and 4 or 5 inches in diameter at the bottom, and about 3½ inches at the top. They are set up and joined together at the top by a pin, and thereby form a triangle upon being opened: the gin is sometimes furnished with a windlass, fixed between two of the legs, and turned by handspikes. The rope is connected with two pulley blocks, and one end is attached to the weight to be lifted, the other passes over the pin, and thence to the windlass.

When a gin is required to be raised, it is laid flat on the ground (the lower end of the single leg extending the contrary way to the others) in order to attach the upper block; and after the rope has been turned round both, the upper end is gradually lifted up.

GIRDER, a name much employed at the present time to both iron and timber beams in whatever situation they may occur, although a girder, properly speaking, is the principal beam of a floor, extending across the building, and a girder employed to carry the superincumbent part of an external wall was formerly distinguished as a bressummer, and generally rested upon oak posts. . . .

GLASS, the material filled in the sash-frames of windows for the purpose of keeping out the rain and wind, and which it effects without excluding the light.

The glass in common use for the windows of houses is first blown in somewhat the shape of a globe, and then flattened in a furnace, and formed into circular plates called *tables,* from 3 feet 6 inches to 4 or 5 feet diameter. The best glass comes from Newcastle and from Bristol. There are three qualities of table glass, which are denominated best, seconds, and thirds. The best is of a good clear colour, and of course the most free from blisters, specks, streaks, flaws, and defects, and the thirds approach a green colour. Plate glass is the best description of glass, and very extensively used for shop windows and superior houses. It is perfectly flat, being cast in plates, and polished. It can be obtained of almost any size. German sheet glass is also of good quality, and can also be had of large dimensions, although it does not look well on the exterior.

GROUNDS, the pieces of wood laid upon the inside faces of walls, to fasten woodwork to; being of similar thickness to the plastering, and consequently flush with it, and nailed to the bond-timber or the plugging. Grounds are also serviceable for strengthening the plaster; for instance, when placed over an aperture. They are usually either grooved or rebated along the edge next the plaster, which is run into it, whereby they key together and the plaster is prevented shrinking away in the drying, and leaving a crack.

GROUT, or GROUTING, a description of mortar used in brick and stone work, consisting of quick lime and a portion of fine sand, employed in a thin semi-liquid state; it is poured into the upper beds and internal joints of the work.

Brickwork should be well grouted every four courses.

GUILLOCH, or GUILLOCHI, a sort of carved ornament, being one or more bands twisted in a variety of ways, and forming a sort of figure, which is repeated throughout the length of the plane on which it is placed, in a similar manner to a fret.

HACKING, an objectional practice in stone walling, occuring when one of the courses of a wall cannot be carried up of equal height throughout for want of stones sufficiently large for same. The hacking consists in dividing the remaining portion into two courses; the end stones being frequently notched to receive the stones of the lesser courses.

HALF-TIMBERED HOUSES, a description of dwelling common to this country about the time of Elizabeth, consisting of strong timber foundations, supports, knees, and studs, filled in with plaster.

HALVING, a mode of securing two pieces of timber together endways, and which is effected by notching a piece out of each at the place of intersection or jointure. It is sometimes called by the name of *halved and spiked;* the piece of wood taken out of each plate extending half through the thickness of the wood, and they are secured together by a spike driven through from the upper surface.

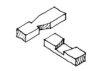

DOVETAILED HALVING

HEADING JOINT (in joinery), the joint formed by the meeting of two boards endways, as in flooring boards and handrails, and which consequently passes transversely across the grain of the wood. It is usual to tongue the headings in

COMMON HALVING

157

BEVELED HALVING

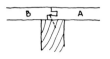

superior floors. The board A is first laid and nailed to the joist, and the board B pushed under afterwards. The headings in oak floors are sometimes formed by toothings.

HEART BOND (in stone walling), a certain description of bond in which there are no through stones; two stones are laid across the wall, which meet in the centre and form the thickness of the wall, and the joint between them is covered by another stone in the course above.

HEWN STONE, a term applied to stone when reduced to the required form, by means of a mallet and chisel only.

HOARDING, the name given to the wooden boarding enclosing any building operations.

HOLLOW WALL, a sort of double wall, or one having a hollow, extending throughout it vertically, for the purpose of saving materials, and as a preventive to damp.

Hollow walls are generally employed for ice houses and wine cellars, to preserve an even temperature, and keep them dry.

HOUSING, the notching out of certain portions in the substance of a piece of wood for the insertion of other pieces; thus, the steps of a staircase are *housed* into the stringboard, and the ends of a pair of rafters are sometimes *housed* into the head of a king-post.

IMPOST, a sort of capping at the top of a pier supporting an arch, and employed for the purpose of receiving the archivolt. A plain square impost is called a *flatband*.

INTERJOIST, a term sometimes used in reference to the space between two joists, which should never be less than 12 inches in the clear.

INTERTIES, or INTERDUCES, the horizontal pieces of timber framed in between posts in roofing, stud-work, partitions, etc. to bind the same together.

IRON CEMENT, a cement for making iron joints, and composed of 16 parts of iron filings free from rust, 3 parts of powdered sal-ammoniac (muriate of ammonia); and 2 parts of flower of sulphur, mixed together, and kept in a stopped vessel until required for use, when to the quantity, represented by 1, must be mixed 12 of clean iron filings, and as much water as will give it the consistency of paste, a few drops of sulphuric acid being previously mixed with the water. If the cement is made entirely of cast iron it is not so tenacious as when formed with wrought iron.

JACK TIMBER, a term applied to any beams that are shortened in length, compared with those which accompany and correspond with them.

JAMBS, the upright sides of any opening, either in a wall or partition, on which the lintel or arch rests.

JAMB POSTS, the posts framed in a partition to fix the jamb linings to.

JAMB STONES (in masonry), the stones employed in building the sides of an aperture, in which case every other course should be in one stone.

JIB DOOR, a door flush with the surface of a wall, and formed with whatever dressings occur in the room upon it, as the base and surbase. Jib doors are adopted for the purpose of concealment.

JOGGLE JOINT, a term applied to a particular description of joint, thus, to the joint connecting two stones, or other bodies, in such a manner that they cannot slip away from each other without tearing the joggle or joint asunder. A separate piece of hard stone, or slate, called a *joggle*, is sometimes introduced at the joints of stones exposed to great strains.

JOINERY, the name given to all finishings in wood work, for the purposes of building, which are framed or fitted together; rough timber-work being called *carpentry*. The stairs, doors, windows and dressings generally come under the head of joinery; also the covering with wood of all rough timber.

JOISTS, COMMON JOISTS, BRIDGING, or BOARDING JOISTS, the timbers employed in naked flooring, for the support of the floor boards, the ceiling also secured to them on the underside. Common joists are sometimes supported by others, termed *binding joists,* and are generally notched down upon them. The distance between joists should not exceed 12 inches, although this is not always strictly abided by.

Common joists should not be employed where the bearing exceeds 16 feet, and it is customary to employ a tier of herring-bone strutting between them, about 6 or 8 feet apart, to prevent their twisting horizontally.

KEY (of a floor), a name sometimes used in reference to the last board laid; the term is also applied to the strutting pieces framed in between the joists in a transverse direction to their sides.

KNOB (glass), the centre part of a table of glass when cut for use.

KNOBBING, the operation of knocking off the rough projections from stone in quarrying, also called *skiffling.*

KNOTTING AND STOPPING, the first process in painting, being the preparatory operation previous to commencing the regular painting; it consists of stopping all nail-holes, cracks, and defects with white lead, and laying a coat of red over the knots, to prevent gum oosing out; a second coat is then spread, consisting of white and red lead and oil, which prevents the knots being distinguished when the painting is finished. A silver leaf is sometimes laid over the knots, with gold size, in superior apartments, which conceals them more effectually.

KYANIZE, a vague term, implying the process to which timber is sometimes subjected for prevention of dry rot. It was invented and patented by Mr. Kyan, and consists of a solution of corrosive sublimate, in which the timber is immersed, whereby the primary element of fermentation is neutralized, and the fibers of the wood rendered indestructible. It also effectually seasons the timber, occupying a space of only two or three months, instead of from two to six years, which is usually required when it is laid to dry after the common method; and it also protects it from the ravages of insects. . . .

LAGGING, a name applied to the narrow planks extending from one rib to another in the centering of arches.

LAID ON, a term applied to a moulding when worked separately, and fastened on a door or other framing, by brads, after the door is put together.

LANDING, the piece of flooring at the head of a flight of stairs.

LANTERN, a sort of tower raised upon a roof for the purpose of giving light below, either circular, square, or polygonal, the sides being occupied by windows. Those in common use are rested upon the walls, and they are distinguished from skylights, by having lights in the sides only, and not upon the top, as with the latter. Lanterns are employed in all styles of modern architecture, and sometimes with considerable effect.

LAP, or BOND (of slate), the distance from the nail of the lower slate to the lower extremity of the upper slate, or the slate lying upon it; the *gage of the slate* being that portion which is open to the weather. The part exposed to view from beneath being called the *margin of the slate*.

LATCH, a sort of temporary fastening to a door, consisting of a hinge bolt, and catch.

LATH, a thin strip of wood, and employed in building for various purposes, but principally in the plastering of ceilings and partitions. Laths are also employed in slating and tiling, and for filleting, furring up, etc.

The laths are commonly of fir at the present time, and consist of split wood, the rending of laths consituting a business. The laths are designated single, lath and half, and double laths, according to their thickness. The first are generally taken at half that of the double, and the lath and half at midway between the two; the single are barely a quarter of an inch thick, and the double three-eighths of an inch, the breadth of each being about one inch.

The laths used in ceilings are required to be of the best kind, those employed for entrance floors, drawing-room floors, and grand staircases, should be double fir laths. Laths are formed in three, four, and five feet lengths; they are also of two qualities, viz., heart laths, and sap laths; the former should always be employed in roofing, and in exposed situations; the second class may be employed in plastering for all common purposes; oak laths, however, should always be used in roofing.

LATH LAID AND SET, the mode of finishing the ceilings and partitions of common houses, being two-coat work. The surfaces of ceilings are whitened, and partitions coloured. The laying, however, is put on without scratching, as in pricking up and roughing in, at least with no more than can be accomplished with a broom.

LATH LAID, SET, and COLOURED, the same as lath laid and set, with the addition of colouring, which is generally applied to the surfaces of walls and partitions.

LATHING (for plastering), the laths employed in plastering are nailed on the quartering or joisting, side by side, and the narrower they are the better, provided they be sufficiently strong to receive the nails, as the greater number of joints are thereby obtained for the plaster to hold or cling to. The nails are formed of cast iron, the joints being broken as much as possible; the laths should not be lapped over one another at the ends, as it occupies a greater thickness, and thereby reduces the substance of the plaster.

LAYING, the operation of laying the first coat of plaster in two coat work, when spread on laths, as applied on ceilings and partitions; the first coat of two-coat work on brickwork being called *rendering*. Both laying and rendering are composed of the same materials, viz., coarse stuff mixed with sand or drift; the surface is swept over with a broom, and not scratched over with a scratcher, as in pricking up and roughing in.

LEAD LIGHTS, a certain mode of filling in window frames. The glass is fixed in lead quarries, and in squares, and they are secured by leaden bands to cross bars, termed *saddle bars,* and are formed of wrought iron. Lead lights are very well suited for ecclesiastic architecture, having been generally employed in ancient Gothic buildings. The portion of the window that opens consists of an iron frame, or casement, to which the lights are fastened, and it is hung upon the window frame, or munnion, as the case may be.

LIME AND HAIR, a mixture of lime and hair, and employed with the plaster in first coats and floating; a greater quantity of hair is used in the latter than in the former. It is also sometimes called *coarse stuff*

LINING, the name given to the boarding covering the interior surface of any-thing. When laid over outside surfaces it is termed *casing*—thus, the inside of walls are sometimes lined to a height of 4 or 5 feet from the floor. Side jambs and soffits are also called *jamb linings* or *linings*.

LISTED BOARDS, a term applied to boards when the sap wood is removed from the edges, which consequently reduces their breadth.

LUFFER BOARDS, a number of boards placed one above the other in an aperture of a tower or lantern, and in slanting direction, for the purpose of excluding rain without presenting impediment to the sound of the bells within, when the latter are rung. Luffer boarding is also frequently employed in factories to pass off smoke and foul vapours.

LUNETTE, an arched aperture cut in the side of a large vault, and of less height than the pitch, for the purpose of admitting light.

MANTLE, a horizontal piece, or lintel, placed on the jambs of a chimney.

MASTIC, an oil cement, invented nearly a century back by Mr. P. Lorist, and for which a patent was subsequently taken out. It is principally employed for coating buildings and floors. It has the power of resisting heat and adhering to iron, copper and glass.

MEZANINE, or MEZZANINE, a low story located between two principal stories.

The word *mezanine*, properly speaking, refers to windows only which are less in height than in width, and occurs in attics as well as in entresoles.

MIDDLE RAIL, the rail situated between the top and bottom rail of a door, when there are no more than three. It should be made level with the hand, as the lock is generally fastened upon it.

MONTANT, a name sometimes given to an upright piece in a frame.

MOSAIC WORK, an ornamental kind of finishing, and adopted for plain surfaces, in interior decoration. It consists of a collection of small pieces of glass, shells, precious stones, marble, and wood of various kinds, cut square, and cemented on a ground of prepared stucco. When wood, stone, or marble is exclusively used, it is called *marquetry*, or *inlaying*.

MOULD, an instrument used by artificers for forming mouldings, etc.; it is cut on the edge to the counter shape of the moulding to be formed. The moulds used by plasterers for running their mouldings are usually edged with metal, great accuracy being required. . . . The term *mould* is likewise used for the beds prepared for any casting, whether of metal or plaster, which contains the pattern embedded upon it.

162

MULLION, or MUNION, a term used in Gothic architecture in reference to the moulded bars which separate the several compartments of windows. They are formed of divers patterns, according to the style. Mullions always stand in a vertical position; those bars lying horizontally are called *transoms*. . . .

NAKED, a term sometimes applied to anything plain or without ornament. It is also employed in another sense—thus, a pilastre projecting 3 inches before the face of a wall, is said to "exceed the *naked* of the wall 3 inches." The *naked* of a wall is the plain surface from whence all projections commence.

NAKED FLOORING, the rough timbering employed in supporting a floor, comprising the joisting; also the binding joists and girders, if there be any; but not the flooring boards. . . . It may be observed, that girders and other beams should always be laid the shortest way across the apartment, and the same remark may be applied to common joists.

NEWEL, the wooden posts situated at the top and bottom of a flight of steps in certain description of staircases, the shafts and supports of the stairs being tenoned into them: that part of the newel next the stairs if formed square, and the remaining portion is usually turned, and hence described as a *turned newel*.

The ornamental cast iron pillars sometimes placed upon the curtail step of a staircase, is likewise called a *newel;* and the circular centre in stone winding stairs, which is formed by the ends of the steps, a *solid newel;* and in open wooden stairs, the circular winding post is called an *open newel,* round which the steps turn.

NOGGING PIECES, the horizontal pieces of timber employed in brick-nog partitions, which are placed about 2 feet apart, and nailed to the quarters, for the purpose of strengthening the brickwork.

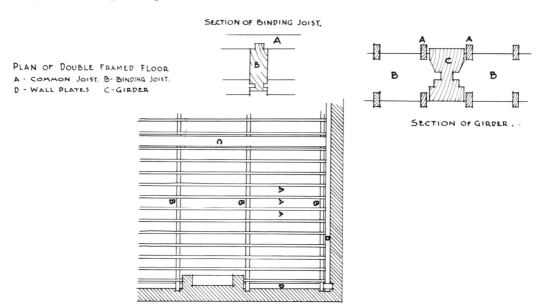

SECTION OF BINDING JOIST.

PLAN OF DOUBLE FRAMED FLOOR
A - COMMON JOIST. B- BINDING JOIST.
D - WALL PLATES   C-GIRDER

SECTION OF GIRDER . -

NOGS, or WOOD BRICKS, blocks of wood the size of a brick, and let into the inside faces of a wall, to fasten the joinery to. The term is also used in reference to square pieces of wood piled up on each side to support the roof of a mine.

NOSING, a small moulded projection occurring on the edges of steps and landings. The nosings of common steps consist of mere rounds, formed on the edges of the treads; but superior stairs have a hollow place beneath the round: the nosings are likewise continued on the ends of the steps, and united at the angles.

NOTCHED BOARD, a board notched or grooved out to receive the end of a flight of steps.

OFFICES (domestic), the name given to that part of a house or mansion occupied principally by the domestics, comprising the kitchen, brew-house, wash-house, pantries, coal and wood-houses.

OFFSET, a sort of ledge occurring in the face of a wall, at the spot where two different thicknesses are connected together, the upper part being parallel to the lower, and receding from it.

ORTHOGRAPHY, a geometrical representation of anything, as an elevation or section of a building.

OUT TO OUT, a term used by workmen in measuring their work, signifying the utmost limits or dimensions of a body.

OVERSAILING, a word used in the same sense as projecting; thus, a cornice projecting 9 inches before the face of the wall, is said to *oversail* 9 inches.

PAINTING, one of the branches of building, and that employed in finishing.

The painting in common use is executed in oil, and three or four coats are sufficient for most purposes. If the work receive any peculiar painting, as graining, or marbling, it is charged extra; flatting is sometimes laid on in ten coats.

Stucco should not be painted until quite dry, which usually comprehends space from one to two years, but when laid on battens and lathing it takes less time. It is therefore customary to colour it in the first instance, which should be well washed off when the painting ultimately takes place.

PARGETING, the lining of walls when formed of plastering, and consisting usually of lime, sand, hair, etc. The term however, is principally employed in reference to the plastering used in coating the internal surfaces of chimneys.

PARPOINT WORK, a description of walling consisting of small squared stones

164

laid in tolerably regular courses, with *through-stones* at intervals of 5 or 6 feet, the whole well grouted.

PARTITION, or QUARTER PARTITION, a thin wall formed of wood framing, and lathed and plastered over. The partitions of houses should, if possible, be placed over walls, for the purpose of support, otherwise recourse must be had to trussing. The bottom plate of a common quarter partition is called a *sill,* that portion of the sill occuring in the opening for the door being cut out, and the upper plate a *head;* the principal uprights, as those on each side of doors, being termed *principal posts,* and the others *quarters;* the raking pieces are called *braces.* Partitions are sometimes constructed of brick and stone.

PATERA, an antique ornament used in friezes, etc., being in the form of a cup; the term, however, is applied to any circular ornament placed in bas relief upon a flat surface.

PAVILION, a name sometimes given to a projecting apartment at the flanks of a building.

PENT ROOF, a roof formed with two equal sloping sides, the extremities forming gables.

PIAZZA, a square open court surrounded by buildings. The name, is however, applied at the present time to such a covered walk, as an arcade, colonnade, etc.

PIEDROIT, a square pier attached to a wall, and differing from pilaster by having neither cap nor base.

PINE (timber), a description of fir imported from America. Good pine opens a bright red colour, and is very free from knots. It is nearly equal to Baltic fir; but yellow pine is not fit for building purposes, although often adopted for panels, mouldings, and other inside purposes.

Canadian timber is frequently cut to the same shape as the Baltic, for the purpose of imposition.

PISE, a material employed in construction walling in some parts of the continent, and occasionally in this country, consisting of stiff earth well beaten and rammed in between moulds prepared of the size of the intended wall. It is finished by rough-cast on the outside, and plaster within.

PLANKING, a term applied to a layer of planks, or to any other timber (excepting fir) when exceeding 1½ inches in thickness.

A deal is 9 inches wide by 3 inches thick; a plank is 11 inches by 3 inches; and flat timber, exceeding these dimensions is called *slabs.*

PLUMBERY, or PLUMBING, one of the trades connected with building. It comprises all works executed in lead, as roofs, gutters, and flats, also pipes, water-closets, cisterns and pumps.

POINTING, a term applied to the finishing of the external face of the several courses of a wall. There are two kinds of pointing. In the first, the mortar is scraped out and then filled up with blue mortar, the courses being simply marked with the edge of the trowel; this is called *flat joint pointing.* In the second, the joints are further finished by fine plaster, which is neatly inserted, and pared to a parallel edge, which slightly projects, and is called *tuck pointing,* or *tuck joint pointing.* This is sometimes performed with Roman cement.

POLYCHROMY, the art of decorating buildings by painting. Nothing illustrates the effect of custom, and the fashion attending everything *sub lunare,* more than the recent discovery that the ancient Greek temples were painted with gaudy colours. The idea of painting white marble is hardly conceivable at the present time (1853).

PORCH, or PORTAL, a sort of covered entrance to a building. A porch consisting of a row of columns is called a *portico.*

PORTICO, a sort of covered colonnade or piazza. The distinction between them consists in a portico being situated at the entrance of a building, while a colonnade piazza surrounds it, or encloses courts and galleries. At least, such is the meaning attached to the words at the present time (1853).

QUARTERS, the vertical timber framing used in partitions to support lath and plaster work. There are two descriptions of quarters made use of; 1st, those placed next the jambs of doors, and at each end of the partition constituting the framework, and which are called *principal* or *double quarters;* 2ndly, the filling-in pieces between the former, which are termed *quarters, common* or *single quarters.* The former are generally sawn to a scantling of 4 inches square, or 4 inches by 2½ or 3 inches, and the latter to about 4 inches by 2 inches. Common quarters should not be placed more than 12 or 14 inches apart.

QUICK LIME, also called caustic lime.

QUOIN, the name given to the corners of stone and brick walls, whether occurring externally or internally, but referring more particularly to the stone edging sometimes employed in brickwork. If the stones project before the face of the wall, and have chamfered edges, they are termed *rustic quoins.*

RAIL, a term much used in carpentry and joinery in reference to any piece of wood laid in a horizontal position; thus, to the horizontal pieces occuring above and below balusters and posts, and hence called railing; those portions of framing surrounding panels which lie in a horizontal position, and receive the tenons of the stiles. The upper and lower rails of a frame are designated as the *top* and *bottom* rails, and if there be an intermediate one it is called the *middle rail.*

RAISING PLATE, the plate upon which the roof directly rests.

RAMP, the concavity on the upper side of a handrail over the risers, and half and quarter spaces arising from the suddeness of the rise. It is frequently necessary to place a knee above a ramp.

RED RUBBER, a description of red brick of similar texture to a malm cutter, and formerly much employed for a like purpose. [*malm cutter not described*]

RENDER, the first coat of plastering in two-coat work when on naked brick or stone. When spread on laths, as for ceilings and partitions, it is called *laid.* The term *render* is sometimes applied to three-coat work, although improperly; thus, *rendered* and *floated* implies three coats, the stuff employed being precisely similar to that used in laying.

REGRATING, a term used by workmen in the same sense as reworking, in reference to the external face of an old hewn stone, which operation gives it the appearance of freshness.

RETICULATED WORK, a name applied when the courses are placed *lozenge wise,* bearing some resemblance to the meshes of a net.

REVEALS, or REVELS, the vertical returns or sides of an aperture. The outside returns of windows and doors are termed *reveals,* and are usually set square with the fade, and 4½ inches in breadth in brick buildings. The inside returns are termed *jambs,* and are sometimes splayed. The reveals of chimneys are usually about 1 foot 2 inches deep, and 1 foot 6 inches in kitchens.

ROD, a long rule employed in setting out and measuring artificers' work. The rod employed in setting out the several parts of a building is generally 10 feet long, but the rods used by measuring surveyors are 5 feet long, and divided into feet and inches, a pair being employed.

ROOD, the fourth part of an acre, equal to 40 square rods, or 1210 square yards.

ROOM, the name given to an apartment generally. The square is the most economical shape for a room, i.e., a given amount of walling will enclose a larger area when laid out in the form of a square than when in a parallelogram. The latter is the most convenient shape, and the circle is the least adapted for apartments generally. The length of a large room should be from one-third to twice that of the width, and small rooms may approach a square form with a less loss of effect than large ones. The height of a room is regulated by the width, without reference to the length. A proportion of three-fourths of the width is quite sufficient where the ceiling is flat; but if it is arched the height should be made at least equal to the width. . . .

ROMAN CEMENT, a cement in very general use for building purposes, being formed of a stone called clay-balls, or septarian limestone. It forms an excellent water cement, and is also a perfect preventive against corrosion, and therefore serviceable in covering joints in ironwork, and other similar purposes. . . .

ROSE, a name sometimes applied to a circular flower occuring in a ceiling, etc.

RUSTIC WORK (wood), an imitation of a primitive mode of building, being rough and simple in appearance, and for which wood is found a very suitable material.

SADDLEBACK, the term applied to the raising of the top joints in stone copings and cornices to carry the water off, the other parts of the stones being sunk lower.

SALOON, a large apartment in a house, and used for a similar purpose to a hall, frequently occupying two stories, with double tiers of windows.

SASH, a thin frame formed with cross bars, and adapted to hold the glass in windows, etc. There are usually two sashes in a window which let up and down by pullies running in different slides. The upper sash occupies the outside slide, and consequently projects slightly before the lower, by which the rain is prevented getting in. The upper sash is sometimes fixed, when the window is described as *single hung,* and when both are hung they are said to be *double hung.* The whole of some sashes are fixed, as those in shop fronts. Sashes sometimes run in grooves sideways, when they are called *sliding sashes.*

The sashes of a window are sometimes hung on hinges like folding doors, one on each side, meeting in the centre, and over-lapping each other. These are known by the name of *French sashes,* and are fastened by long vertical rods or laths. . . .

SAW PIT, an oblong hole in which timber is sawn up, being usually dug in the earth, and edged with wood. The operation of sawing is performed by two men, styled *sawyers,* who do not undertake any other department in building.

168

SCAGLIOLA, a costly description of plastering introduced into this country by the late Mr. Henry Holland, Architect, consisting of an imitation of marble, precious stones, etc. It is very hard, takes a beautifully polished surface, and is exceedingly like marble in appearance, so that it is very frequently employed along with it for the plain parts.

SCHEME, or SKENE ARCH, a circular arch, whose dimensions are not greater than a semicircle.

SKEW-BACK (of a window), the sloping abutment on each side of the arched head of a window.

SKIFFLING, a term applied to the process of knocking off the rough projections of Kentish rag stone at the time of quarrying. It is called knobbing in most other parts.

SKIRTING, the narrow edging laid round the walls of rooms, being scribed or fixed edgways upon it, and consisting of a plinth, either moulded or plain. The skirting of superior rooms is tongued into the floor—see cut—but that for common purposes is merely scribed to the floor, and nailed to fillets at the back. Mr. Hoskins, Architect, suggests that a fillet nailed around a floor, would answer all the purposes of a skirting, and be more cleanly as well as fireproof. Any mouldings, by way of ornament, might be run in plaster over it.

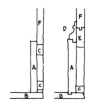

SKIRTING

A SKIRTING BOARD
B FLOOR
C FILLETS
D BASE MOULDING
E NARROW GROUNDS
F PLASTERING

SPLAYED, sometimes called Fluing, a term signifying anything that is formed diagonally, as the jambs of gothic windows and other apertures, and the heading joints of floor boards.

STEINING, the operation of lining a well with bricks. The wall is first carried up a certain height from the ground, upon a strong curb, the workmen digging out the ground on the inside, and eventually from beneath the ring itself, upon which the whole sinks from the effect of gravity.

The brickwork is carried up as it is lowered, and if any bricks should be added below, on account of the shaft refusing to descend any lower, such process is termed *underpinning*.

STILES, the vertical pieces of boarding employed in framings, which are morticed to receive the tenons of the rails, and grooved for the panels.

STUD PARTITION, a *Quarter Partition*.

STUD WORK, the same as *Brick-Nogging*.

STUFF, a general name given to the wood used in joinery. . . .

TABLET, or TABLE, a general name for any narrow flat surface, either recessed or projecting; thus, we have raised tables, sunk tables, water tables, etc. The coping of houses is called *tabling* in Scotland.

TAIL BAYS, a name given to common joists when one end is framed in a girder and the other rests on a wall.

TAIL TRIMMER, a trimmer lying by the side of a chimney jamb, and employed to receive the ends of the joists when they cannot be inserted into the wall on account of flues, etc.

TEMPLATE, or TEMPLET, a sort of mould employed in cutting and setting masonry in brickwork. A template consists of a thin piece of iron, cut to the exact section of the moulding or other feature to be worked.

TERRACE, a raised area or walk before a house. Terraces are sometimes formed on the roofs of one portion of a building which are consequently made flat for that purpose.

THROAT, or GORGE, a small semi-circular sinking made on the underside of some projected moulding, etc. Coping sills are mostly *throated*.

TRELLIS WORK, a sort of framing formed of laths, and generally placed diagonally, and used as an enclosure for the purpose of training creepers in rustic erections.

TRIM, TRIM UP, TRIM IN, and TRIM OUT, terms signifying the fitting of one piece of wood between two others already fixed in, in whatever position they may lie; thus a joist is sometimes *trimmed* between two others, and is therefore termed a trimmer; a partition is *trimmed up* between a floor and a ceiling; a post between two beams, etc.

VALLEY, the internal angle formed by the junction of two inclined sides of a roof.

VENEER, a thin piece of mahogany, or other ornamental wood, employed in covering inferior stuff for the purpose of decoration.

VENETIAN DOOR, a door with a small window upon each side, of the same height with it.

VENTILATION (of buildings), the means employed in introducing a fresh supply of air to the several apartments of a building, in passing it through and in forcing it out again when required.

It is strange the little that has been done in a way of ventilation, if we except the recent labours of Drs. Reid and Arnott, and the warm air apparatus; air holes in the floor and flues comprehending all that is usual. . . .

VENTILATOR, a contrivance for passing off foul air from a room, being generally of a circular form.

VESTIBULE, an antehall, lobby, or porch.

WAINSCOTING, the wooden framed linings applied to the walls of apartments. It is but little employed at the present time, although formerly in general use. A preference is now given to plastering on account of its fire-proof qualities, and for the sake of economy. Wainscoting is principally employed in halls, also public and private offices. It generally consists of panelling about five or six feet high; such as is only 3 feet or 3 feet 6 inches is called *dwarf wainscoting*. The joints of wainscoting should be primed at the back to protect the glue from the damp.

WATER-CLOSET, a convenience of a private nature, and connected with all modern dwellings, detached privies being seldom adopted excepting for country residences. When a water-closet is required in the inside of a house, it should, if possible, communicate with a gallery or passage, and be set out on the outside face of the wall, and either supported by walls carried up from below or on corbels, and it should also possess a lobby; it will thus be easy of access, yet private and retired.

WATER TABLE, a name given to a sort of offset occurring on the external face of a wall.

WEATHER BOARDING, the boarding employed in covering outhouses and buildings of a temporary nature. It generally consists of feather-edged boards, the thick part of one board lying over the thin edge of that next it, nails being driven through the top into the quartering at the back.

WEIGHTS, (of sash frames), the cast iron weights used to balance the sashes of windows.

WELL HOLE, called also Hollow newel (in staircases), the opening in the middle of all winding and open staircases.

WHICKET, or WICKET-DOOR, a small door formed in a gate.

WITHS, the partitions dividing the flues of a chimney, which are half a brick thick.

WOOD BRICK: (called Dooks, in Scotland), the small blocks of wood of the same size as bricks, and built in walls on the inside face for the purpose of affording a hold to the woodwork laid against the same.

WROUGHT, the term used in contradistinction to rough, and applied to woodwork when brought to a fair surface, being planed on the sides and edges. The description or assortment of the stuff generally accompanies the term, as "deal wrought," "fir wrought," etc. The term, as applied to masonry, refers to the dressing given to the blocks of freestone after being squared, and previous to their being set in the wall. It is usually performed by a mallet and chisel, and finished off smooth and true by scraping and rubbing.

XYSTOS, a long piazza or walk, either covered or uncovered.

YORKSHIRE STONE, or GRIT, a name sometimes given to Bramley Fall stone; it is one of the most general of the sandstones which are sent to London and is used for paving, copings, and other rough work.

ZOPHORUS, that member of an entablature which is situated between the architrave and cornice, and which usually consists of one entire flat surface — a Frieze.

BIBLIOGRAPHY

This is not intended as a complete bibliography, although it is hoped that most of the important titles have been included. The section on "Regional Characteristics" is suggestive only, since the great number of possible titles necessitated moderation in listing.

Bibliographies

HISTORIC American Buildings Survey, *Historic American Buildings Survey; Catalog of the Measured Drawings and Photographs of the Survey in the Library of Congress, March 1, 1941.* [2nd ed.] Washington, U. S. Govt. Print. Off., 1941. 470 p., illus. — *Catalog Supplement,* Washington, National Park Service, 1959. unp., illus.

HITCHCOCK, Henry-R., *American Architectural Books; a List of Books, Portfolios, and Pamphlets on Architecture and Related Subjects Published in America before 1895,* Minneapolis, University of Minnesota Press, 1946. 130 p., index. (Reprinted 1962, with new preface with a few additions and corrections.)

PARK, Helen, "A List of Architectural Books Available in America before the Revolution," *Journal of the Society of Architectural Historians* 20:115-130, Oct. 1961. illus.

ROOS, Frank J., *Writings on Early Architecture; an Annotated List of Books and Articles on Architecture Constructed before 1860 in the Eastern Half of the United States,* Columbus, Ohio State University Press, 1943. 271 p., index.

For other bibliographies, the reader is referred to the balance of this list, the existence of a bibliography having been noted for each entry.

Dictionaries

ARCHITECTURAL Publication Society, *The Dictionary of Architecture,* London, T. Richards; Whiting and Co., [1853] - 1892. 11 v. illus.

ISHAM, Norman M., *A Glossary of Colonial Architectural Terms, with Illustrations,* The Walpole Society, 1939. 37 p., illus.

SAYLOR, Henry H., *Dictionary of Architecture,* New York, John Wiley and Sons, 1952. 221 p., illus.

WEALE, John, *Rudimentary Dictionary of Terms Used In Architecture, Civil, Architecture, Naval, Building and Construction, Early and Ecclesiastical Art, Engineering, Civil, Engineering, Mechanical, Fine Art, Mining, Surveying, etc., to Which Are Added Explanatory Observations on Numerous Subjects Connected with Practical Art and Science,* London, J. Weale, 1849-50. 564 p., illus.

Archaeology

CAYWOOD, Louis R., *Excavations at Green Spring Plantation,* Yorktown, Va., Colonial National Historical Park, 1955, 29 p., illus., bibliography (Cover title: *Green Spring Plantation, Archeological Report.* Prepared for Virginia 305th Anniversary Commission and Jamestown-Williamsburg-Yorktown-Celebration Commission).

COLONIAL Williamsburg, Inc., *The President's Report, 1960,* [n. p., 1960?] 63 p., illus.

HAMMOND, Philip C., *Archaeological Techniques for Amateurs,* Princeton, N.J., D. Van Nostrand Co., 1963. 329 p. illus., bibliography, index.

NOEL Hume, Ivor, *Excavations at Rosewall in Gloucester County, Virginia, 1957-1959,* Washington, Smithsonian Institution, 1962. p. 153-229, illus. (U. S. National Museum. Bulletin 225 [pt. 7]—Contributions from the Museum of History and Technology. Paper 18.)

NOEL Hume, Ivor, *Here Lies Virginia; an Archaeologist's View of Colonial Life and History,* New York, Knopf, 1963, 316 p., illus., bibliography, index.

ROBBINS, Roland W. and Evan Jones, *Hidden America,* New York, Knopf, 1959. 263 p., illus., bibliography, index.

Architectural History

ANDREWS, Wayne, *Architecture in America; a Photographic History from the Colonial Period to the Present,* New York, Atheneum Publishers, 1960. 179 p., illus., index.

COLES, William A. and Henry H. Reed, ed. *Architecture in America: a Battle of Styles,* New York, Appleton-Century-Crofts, 1961. 412 p., illus., bibliography, glossary

FLETCHER, Sir Banister F., *A History of Architecture on the Comparative Method,* 17th ed., rev. by R. A. Cordingley, New York, C. Scribner's Sons, 1961. 1366 p., illus., bibliography, glossary, index.

GUTHEIM, Frederick A., *One Hundred Years of Architecture in America, 1857-1957,* New York, Reinhold Publishing Corp., 1957. 96 p., illus.

HAMLIN, Talbot F., *Greek Revival Architecture in America: Being an Account of Important Trends in American Architecture and American Life Prior to the War Between the States,* London, New York, Oxford University Press, 1944. 439 p., illus., biblography, index..

HITCHCOCK, Henry-R., *Architecture, Nineteenth and Twentieth Centuries,* Baltimore, Penguin Books, 1958. 498 p., illus., bibliography, index.

HITCHCOCK, Henry-R., *The Architecture of H. H. Richardson and His Times,* [Rev. ed.], Hamden, Conn., Archon Books, 1961. 343 p., illus., bibliography, index.

KIMBALL, Sidney F., *American Architecture,* Indianapolis and New York, Bobbs-Merrill Co., 1928. 262 p., illus., bibliography, index.

LANCASTER, Clay, *Architectural Follies in America; or, Hammer, Saw-tooth & Nail,* Rutland Vt., C. E. Tuttle Co. 1960. 243 p., illus., bibliographical footnotes, index.

MAASS, John, *The Gingerbread Age; a View of Victorian America,* New York, Rinehart, 1957. 212 p., illus., bibliography, index.

MC CALLUM, Ian R. M., *Architecture USA,* New York, Reinhold Publishing Corp., 1959. 216 p., illus., bibliography.

SCULLY, Vincent J., *The Shingle Style; Architectural Theory and Design from Richardson to the Origins of Wright,* New Haven, Yale University Press, 1955. 181 p., illus., bibliography, index.

Regional Characteristics

ARCHITECTS' Emergency Committee, *Great Georgian Houses of America,* New York, Kalkhoff Press, 1933-37. 2 v., illus.

BAILEY, Rosalie F., *Pre-Revolutionary Dutch Houses and Families in Northern New Jersey and Southern New York,* New York, W. Morrow & Co., 1936. 612 p., illus., bibliography, index.

BAIRD, Joseph A., *Time's Wondrous Changes: San Francisco Architecture, 1776-1915,* San Francisco, California Historical Society, 1962. 67 p., illus., bibliography, glossary, index.

BRIGGS, Martin S., *The Homes of the Pilgrim Fathers in England and America (1620-1685),* London and New York, Oxford University Press, 1932. 211 p., illus., bibliography, index.

DEAS, Alston, *The Early Ironwork of Charleston,* Columbia, S. C., Bostick and Thornley, 1941. 111 p., illus., bibliography, index.

DE LAGERBERG, Lars, *New Jersey Architecture, Colonial & Federal,* Springfield, Mass., W. Whittum, 1956. v. p., illus. index.

EBERLEIN, Harold D. and C. V. D. Hubbard, *Historic Houses and Buildings of Delaware,* Dover, Delaware, Public Archives Commission, 1963. 227 p., illus., index.

FORMAN, Henry C., *The Architecture of the Old South: The Medieval Style, 1585-1850,* Cambridge, Harvard University Press, 1948. 203 p., illus., bibliography, index.

FRARY, Ihna T., *Early Homes of Ohio,* Richmond, Garrett and Massie, 1936. 336 p., illus., bibliography, index.

The GEORGIAN Period; a Collection of Papers Dealing with "Colonial" or XVIII-Century Architecture in the United States, Boston, American Architect and Building News Co., 1899-1902. 3 v., illus.

HAMMOND, Ralph C., *Ante-Bellum Mansions of Alabama,* New York, Architectural Book Publishing Co., 1951. 196 p., illus., index.

HANNAFORD, Donald R. and Revel Edwards, *Spanish Colonial or Adobe Architecture of California, 1800-1850,* New York, Architectural Book Publishing Co., 1931. 110 p., illus.

ISHAM, Norman M. and Albert F. Brown, *Early Connecticut Houses; an Historical and Architectural Study,* Providence, R.. I., Preston and Rounds Co., 1900. 303 p., illus., index.

KELLY, John F., *Early Connecticut Architecture; Measured Drawings with Full Size Details of Moulded Sections.* 1st. & 2nd series. New York, W. Helburn, Inc., 1924-1931. 2 v. illus.

KELLY, John F., *The Early Domestic Architecture of Connecticut,* New Haven, Yale University Press, 1924. 210 p., illus., index.

KIMBALL, Sidney F., *Domestic Architecture of the American Colonies and of the Early Republic,* New York, C. Scribner's Sons, 1922. 314 p., illus., bibliographical footnotes, index.

LANCASTER, Clay, *Old Brooklyn Heights: New York's First Suburb,* Rutland, Vt., C. E. Tuttle Co., 1961. 183 p., illus., bibliography, glossary, index.

The MONOGRAPH Series, Records of Early American Architecture. v. 1-26, New York, 1915-1940. illus. (v. 1-14 The White Pine Series of Architectural Monographs).

MORRISON, Hugh S., *Early American Architecture, from the First Colonial Settlements to the National Period,* New York, Oxford University Press, 1952. 619 p., illus., bibliography, index.

NEWCOMB, Rexford, *Architecture of the Old Northwest Territory; a Study of Early Architecture in Ohio, Indiana, Illinois, Michigan, Wisconsin & Part of Minnesota,* Chicago, University of Chicago Press, 1950. 175 p. xcvi pl., illus., bibliography, glossary, index.

NEWCOMB, Rexford, *Old Kentucky Architecture, Colonial, Federal, Greek Revival, Gothic, and Other Types Erected Prior to the War Between the States,* New York, W. Helburn, Inc., 1940. 154 p., illus.

NEWCOMB, Rexford, *Spanish-Colonial Architecture in the United States,* New York, J. J. Augustin, 1937. 170 p., illus.

PEAT, Wilbur D., *Indiana Houses of the Nineteenth Century,* Indianapolis, Indiana Historical Society, 1962. 195 p., illus., index.

PERRIN, Richard W. E., [Series of Articles on Wisconsin Architecture] *Wisconsin Magazine of History* 63(4), Summer 1960 to 68(1) Fall 1964. ilus., bibliographical footnotes. (Appeared in most issues of period indicated).

PHILADELPHIA Art Alliance, *Philadelphia Architecture in the Nineteenth Century,* Theo B. White, ed., Philadelphia, Univ. of Pennsylvania Press, 1953. 36, [86] p., illus.

RAYMOND, Eleanor, *Early Domestic Architecture of Pennsylvania,* New York, W. Helburn, 1931. 182 p., illus.

RICCIUTI, Italo W., *New Orleans and Its Environs; the Domestic Architecture, 1727-1870,* New York, W. Helburn, Inc., 1938. 160 p., illus.

STOTZ, Charles M., *The Early Architecture of Western Pennsylvania, a Record of Building before 1860,* New York, W. Helburn, Inc., 1936. 290 p., illus., bibliography, index.

TALLMADGE, Thomas E., *Architecture in Old Chicago,* Chicago, University of Chicago Press, 1941. 218 p., illus., index.

WATERMAN, Thomas T. and John A. Barrows, *Domestic Colonial Architecture of Tidewater Virginia*, New York, C. Scribner's Sons, 1932. 191 p., illus., glossary, index.

WATERMAN, Thomas T., *The Dwellings of Colonial America*, Chapel Hill, University of North Carolina Press, 1950. 312 p., illus., bibliography, glossary, index.

WATERMAN, Thomas T., *The Mansions of Virginia, 1706-1776*, Chapel Hill, University of North Carolina Press, 1946. 456 p., illus., bibliography, glossary, index.

Handbooks

BENJAMIN, Asher, *The Practical House Carpenter. Being a Complete Development of the Grecian Orders of Architecture* . . . 2d ed., Boston, S. Walker, 1830. 119 p., illus., glossary.

BENJAMIN, Asher, *Practice of Architecture. Containing the Five Orders of Architecture, and an Additional Column and Entablature* . . . 2d ed., Boston, B. B. Mussey, 1835. 116 p., illus.

BROWN, William, *The Carpenter's Assistant: Containing a Succinct Account of Egyptian, Grecian and Roman Architecture* . . . *Revised, Improved, and Enlarged, with Additions on Rural Architecture* . . . *by Lewis E. Joy* . . . Boston, E. Livermore, 1854. 148 p., illus., glossary.

GIBBS, James, *Rules for Drawing the Several Parts of Architecture, in a More Exact and Easy Manner Than Has Been heretofore Practiced, by Which All Fractions, in Dividing the Principal Members and Their Parts, Are Avoided*, London, Printed by W. Bowyer, for the Author, 1732. 42 p., 64 plates.

SLOAN, Samuel, *Sloan's Homestead Architecture, Containing Forty Designs for Villas, Cottages, and Farm Houses, with Essays on Style, Construction, Landscape Gardening, Furniture, etc., etc.*, 3rd ed., Philadelphia, J. B. Lippincott & Co., 1870. 355 p., illus.

VAUX, Calvert, *Villas and Cottages; a Series of Designs Prepared for Execution in the United States*, New York, Harper & Brothers, 1857. 318 p., illus.

Restoration and Preservation

BRAUN, Hugh, *The Restoration of Old Houses*, London, Faber and Faber, 1954. 192 p., illus., glossary, index.

COBBLESTONE Society, *Preservation & Restoration of Cobblestone Architecture* [Albion, New York, 1964] portfolio, illus.

CONGDON, Herbert W., *Early American Homes for Today; a Treasury of Decorative Details and Restoration Procedures,* Rutland, Vt., C. E. Tuttle Co., 1963. 236 p., illus., glossary, index.

GILCHRIST, Agnes, *A Primer on the Care and Repair of Buidings,* [Mt. Vernon, N.Y. 1963] 4 p.—(Available from National Trust for Historic Preservation).

"HISTORIC Building Restoration," *Architectural and Engineering News* 6 (6): 74-81, June, 1964. illus.

HOSMER, Charles B. Jr., *Presence of the Past; A history of the preservation movement in the United States before Williamsburg,* New York, G. P. Putnam's Sons, 1965. 386 p., illus., bibliography, index.

INSALL, Donald W., *The Care of Old Buildings; a Practical Guide for Architects and Owners,* London, Society for the Protection of Ancient Buildings, 1958. 73 p., illus., bibliography.

KELLY, John F., *The Henry Whitfield House, 1639. The Journal of the Restoration of The Old Stone House, Guilford,* Guilford, Conn., The Henry Whitfield State Historical Museum, 1939. 60 p., illus.

KIMBALL, Sidney F., "The Preservation Movement in America," *Journal of The American Society of Architectural Historians* 1 (3/4): 15-17 July/ Oct. 1941.

MERCER, Henry C., *The Dating of Old Houses,* a Paper Read at a Meeting of The Bucks County Historical Society, October 13, 1923. n.p., n.d. 28 p., illus. (Reprinted from a *Collection of Papers Read before The Bucks County Historical Society,* 5:536-549).

MOSES, Robert, "Some Hard Facts about Practical Preservation," *Journal of the American Society of Architectural Historians.* 1(¾): 31-32 July/ Oct. 1941.

NATIONAL Research Council, Prevention of Deterioration Center, *Deterioration of Materials: Causes and Preventive Techniques,* New York, Reinhold Publishing Corp., 1954. 835 p., illus., bibliography, index.

NATIONAL Trust for Historic Preservation, *Publications: National Trust and Other,* Washington, nd. 4 p.

NEWMAN (Rockwell) Co., Orange, New Jersey, *Permanent Restoration of Historic American Buildings; Ten Examples of How the Rockwell Newman Company Restores and Preserves Masonry,* Orange, New Jersey, 1956. 32 p., illus.

179

PATTERSON, Mary S. (Mrs. Henry C.), Escaping Pitfalls in Early Penn-sylvania Restoration," *Daughters of the American Revolution Magazine* 98:240-243+ March 1964. illus.

RIGGS, John B., *Documentary Sources for Historic Preservation: Manuscripts,* Washington, National Trust for Historic Preservation, nd. 4 p., bibliography.

SEABURY, Joseph S., *New Homes under Old Roofs,* New York, Frederick A. Stokes Co., 1916. 95 p., illus.

U. S. NATIONAL Park Service, Division of Design and Construction, Eastern Office, *Nail Chronology as an Aid to Dating Old Buildings; Paint Color Research and Restoration,* Madison, Wis., American Association for State and Local History, 1963. 4 p., illus. (AASLH Technical Leaflet 15). (Authors of papers are Nail—Lee H. Nelson; Paint—Penelope Hartshorne).

Some Other Useful Titles

BILLINGTON, John, *The Architectural Director: Being a Guide to Builders, Draughtsmen, Students, and Workmen, in the Study, Design, and Execution of Architecture . . . and a Glossary of Architecture . . .* 2d ed., Greatly Enl., London, Henry G. Bohn, 1848. 344, 105 p., illus., glossary.

HISTORIC-House Keeping Course, 1955, Cooperstown, New York, *Primer for Preservation: a Handbook for Historic-House Keeping,* n. p., 195-? 23 p., illus. (Articles by F. L. Rath, E. P. Alexander, N. F. Little, F. D. Nichols, F. M. Montgomery, K. Chorley).

MC CLELLAND, Nancy V., *Historic Wall-papers, from Their Inception to the Introduction of Machinery,* Philadelphia, J. B. Lippincott Co., 1924. 458 p., illus., bibliography, index.

MERCER, Henry C., *Ancient Carpenters' Tools, Together with Lumbermen's, Joiners' and Cabinetmakers' Tools in Use in the Eighteenth Century,* Doylestown, Pa., Bucks County Historical Society, 1951. 399 p., illus. bibliography, index.

RAINS, Albert and HENDERSON, Laurance G., *With Heritage So Rich; A report of a Special Committee on Historic Preservation under the auspices of the United States Conference of Mayors with a grant from the Ford Foundation,* New York, Random House, 1966. 230 p., illus., bibliography, index. The book was written by the following authors; Mrs. Helen Duprey Bullock, Carl Feiss, Robert R. Garvey, Jr., Richard H. Howland, Sidney

Hyman, Christopher Tunnard, Walter Muir Whitehill, and George Zabriskie. The Foreword was written by Mrs. Lyndon B. Johnson. There are 218 photographic illustrations 29 of which are in full color.

U. S. NATIONAL Park Service, Division of Design and Construction, Eastern Office, *Manual of the Historic American Buildings Survey, Part IX, Measured Drawings,* Rev. illus., draft compiled by Harley McKee. [Phila., 1961]. 109 p., illus.